ESSENTIAL 100

For Anna, Matthew and Stephanie

ESSENTIAL 100

Your journey through the Bible in 100 readings

Whitney T Kuniholm

ESSENTIAL 100

Published in the UK by Scripture Union, 207–209 Queensway, Bletchley, MK2 2EB, England.

🕊 *Scripture Union:* We are an international Christian charity working with churches in more than 130 countries providing resources to bring the good news about Jesus Christ to children, young people and families – and to encourage them to develop spiritually through the Bible and prayer. As well as our network of volunteers, staff and associates who run holidays, church-based events and school Christian groups, we produce a wide range of publications and support those who use our resources through training programmes.

Email: info@scriptureunion.org.uk

Internet: www.scriptureunion.org.uk

Scripture Union Australia: Locked Bag 2, Central Coast Business Centre, NSW 2252 www.su.org.au

First published 2003 in hardback: ISBN 1 84427 012 2, reprinted 2004.
Published in this Share the Light edition in 2004: ISBN 1 84427 103 X.
Reprinted 2004, 2005.
Published in this E100 edition in 2010: ISBN 978 1 84427 566 3.
Reprinted 2010, 2011

British Library Cataloguing-in-Publication Data: a catalogue record for this book is available from the British Library.

Cover design by Heather Knight.

Internal design and typesetting by Servis Filmsetting Ltd of Manchester.

Printed and bound in Great Britain by Bell & Bain Ltd, Glasgow.

CONTENTS

This special edition of **Essential 100** has been produced as a resource for the E100 Bible Reading Challenge. This is based around 100 carefully selected Bible readings (50 from the Old Testament and 50 from the New Testament) designed to give participants a good understanding of the overall Bible story from Genesis to Revelation. The 'E' stands for Essential and each of the **Essential 100** readings ranges from a few verses to a few chapters.

The programme is very flexible and can be used by individuals or groups in the context of the local church.

We hope completing the E100 Challenge will encourage you to continue spending regular time with God through Bible reading and prayer.

MEET THE AUTHOR OF ESSENTIAL 100

Whitney Kuniholm lives in Exton, Pennsylvania. He and his wife Carol attend an Episcopal church where Whitney is involved in prayer ministry, two small fellowship groups for men and occasional teaching and preaching.

Whitney is the President of Scripture Union in the USA, a position he has held since 1997. In this role, he gives leadership to SU's ministry throughout the United States, which includes evangelism and discipleship programmes for children and young people, as well as the promotion of daily Bible reading and prayer among people of all ages.

When he's not working or writing, Whitney enjoys being with his family, golf, running, or working out at the YMCA. He's a fan of Starbucks coffee, classical, bluegrass and jazz music, and National Public Radio. He also finds time somehow to get involved as a volunteer at an inner city shelter for homeless women and their children called the St Barnabas Mission.

INTRODUCING ESSENTIAL 100

'I've tried to read the Bible but I've never made it all the way through.'

'I've read bits of the Bible but I don't really know how they all fit together.'

'I've never read the Bible – but I'm interested in finding out what's in it.'

'I love the Bible. I just need a little help understanding how it applies to my life today.'

The Bible is the world's most important book. It has sold more copies than any other volume in history. It is the reference point for both the Jewish and Christian religions. And it has affected the culture, law, art and morality of nearly every society on earth.

But the Bible is more than just an influential book. It is the historical record of the most important story of all time: God's interaction with humankind. Although the Bible contains many kinds of writing and introduces us to a wide variety of characters, they all combine to tell one main story, that God created the world, that humans rebelled against God, and that God initiated a plan to save the world – a plan that culminated in Jesus Christ. That's 'the big story' that makes sense of the Bible and all of life.

Essential 100 is a way for you to discover that 'big story' for yourself. It takes you on a journey through 100 easy-to-read passages, organised into 20 sections, so you'll see how all the pieces fit together. Along the way, it gives you opportunities to record your insights and come to your own conclusions on how the Bible's message applies to you today – to connect your story to the 'big story'.

A road map Before you get started on your journey through the Bible, it may help to have a road map. So here's a brief description of how the 20 sections in your study fit into the 'big story' – God's plan of salvation.

The Old Testament

In the beginning The Bible introduces us to its main character – God – in the very first sentence. God's first action is to create a beautiful and intricate world into which he places people, made 'in his own image'. Unfortunately, it doesn't take long for the first people, Adam and Eve, to do wrong and become separated from God. That sets up life's greatest dilemma: how can imperfect and sinful men and women be reconciled to a holy and perfect God?

Abraham, Isaac and Jacob Fortunately, God takes the initiative for solving the dilemma. His first step is to begin a close relationship with one group of people. The three men Abraham, Isaac and Jacob, sometimes called the Patriarchs, are chosen by God to give birth to this special group of people – the Israelites.

7

The story of Joseph The Bible spends a long time on the story of this one man and his family. At first, it appears as though God's plan to create a special nation has been derailed when Joseph is sold as a slave and imprisoned in Egypt. But, in fact, it is in Egypt that 'the chosen people' expand from a family into a nation.

Moses and the Exodus Eventually, the Egyptians begin to oppress the Israelites, so God chooses Moses to lead his people to freedom. In the process, God demonstrates his awesome power and teaches the people important lessons about trusting and obeying him. This rescue, known as the Exodus, also becomes a symbol of a greater freedom God was to offer to all people – freedom from the hold of sin.

The Law and the land Years earlier, God had promised to give Abraham's descendents a land of their own. Moses guides the people through the desert and brings them to the very edge of the Promised Land. But it is Joshua who finally leads the people across the Jordan River and into the land of Canaan. Along the way, God reveals how he wants his people to live, giving them the Ten Commandments.

The judges The Israelites have now become a nation and have entered the Promised Land, but they have no king. Instead, God gives them a variety of 'interim leaders', called judges, whose main responsibility is to save the people from the surrounding enemies. As we read these exciting stories, we learn the consequences of disobedience as well as God's response when his people cry out and return to him.

The rise of Israel God eventually gives Israel a king, Saul, who starts well but in the end is rejected by God for his disobedience. Saul is succeeded by David, the boy who defeats a giant and becomes a national hero. As a result of David's military victories and spiritual passion, Israel reaches a high point in its history and King David becomes a symbol of a much greater king to come – Jesus Christ.

The fall of Israel Although King Solomon is remembered for his wisdom and incredible achievements, he also opened the door – just a little – to idolatry, at the end of his reign. Over time, this small compromise causes the people to wander far away from God and to worship the false gods of surrounding nations. Israel's idolatry leads to a devastating punishment.

Psalms and Proverbs Psalms is a book of prayer and praise, written mostly by David. It provides a window into the inner life of a person the Bible describes as 'a man after God's own heart'. Proverbs is a collection of the sayings, primarily from Solomon, that contain practical wisdom for living a godly life.

The prophets Throughout the history of Israel, God sends prophets who have the difficult task of pronouncing judgement on the idolatry and sin of the people. The prophets also predict the coming of a Messiah. As the Old Testament comes to a close, we are still waiting for the most wonderful part of God's plan to unfold.

The New Testament

The living Word What God had been saying throughout the history of Israel, through signs and wonders and through the Law and the prophets, he now says in person. As the apostle John said, 'So the Word became human and lived here on earth among us' (John 1:14). Jesus Christ was a living, breathing statement of God's love for the world.

The teachings of Jesus Jesus communicates his message to the crowds using sermons and stories drawn from real life (parables). In his most famous sermon, the Sermon on the Mount, Jesus builds on the Law of Moses and explains with incredible insight how God intends us to live. And in the parables, Jesus memorably describes one of the central themes of his teaching – the kingdom of God.

The miracles of Jesus The four Gospels record many of the miracles Jesus performs during his public ministry. He heals the sick, overrules the laws of nature, casts out demons and returns the dead to life. His miracles are not only a demonstration of his compassion and power, they are also proof that he is who he claims to be – the Son of God.

The cross of Christ The main reason Jesus comes to earth is to pay the penalty a perfect God requires for our sin, and offer salvation to all who believe in him. He does this by his death and resurrection. The cross of Christ is at the heart of God's plan of salvation. It is the way he resolves 'the great dilemma' of disobedience, enabling anyone to have a relationship with him. That's the Good News of Christianity!

The Church is born After Jesus' resurrection, he returns to heaven but sends a 'greater gift' – the Holy Spirit. This marks the birth of the Church. In addition, it initiates a dramatic expansion in God's plan of salvation. Ever since Abraham, God has been relating to one group of people, the Israelites. But now the door of salvation is open to everyone.

The travels of Paul The most energetic ambassador of the early Church is the apostle Paul. Originally Paul is a bitter enemy of the Church. But God dramatically turns him around on the Damascus Road and transforms him into a fearless witness for Christ. Paul's missionary journeys are recorded in the Book of Acts and are a major reason why the gospel begins to spread throughout world.

Paul to the churches Paul writes letters to the new believers in churches he started. In them he explains the gospel, encourages believers to grow in their walk with God and offers practical help for living the Christian life. They are as relevant today as they were 2,000 years ago.

Paul to the leaders Paul knows that if the Church is to grow, it needs capable leaders to carry on after him. Therefore, some of his letters are written to instruct church leaders and to warn against false teachers. Since the Church is the way God will continue expanding his plan of salvation in the world until Jesus returns, faithful leadership was vitally important. It still is.

The apostles' teaching In addition to Paul, other apostles like Peter, James and John write letters to encourage and instruct the early followers of Jesus. The letters help us understand different aspects of the gospel and the Christian life. They also provide us with some of the most memorable passages in the Bible.

Revelation Near the end of his life (around 95 AD), the apostle John has a spectacular vision. Through it, God reveals specific messages to seven first-century churches. These messages are still highly applicable to churches in the twenty-first century. Finally, John's vision predicts and describes Christ's return, when God's plan of salvation will reach its ultimate fulfilment.

Using Essential 100

Essential 100 takes you on a journey through the Bible in 100 readings, each of which is one or two chapters in length. (Only 18 readings are longer than two chapters.) The readings are undated so you can complete them at your own pace, though one a day or five a week would be ideal in terms of you gaining a meaningful overview of the Bible.

Essential 100 is designed to be used alongside a Bible. I recommend that before you begin **Essential 100** you find a Bible that is easy for you to read. Although the traditional King James Version is a beautiful and widely available translation, it is often difficult for readers of today to understand, since it was translated into the language of four centuries ago. I recommend you use one of the many excellent newer translations such as the New International Version (NIV), New Living Translation (NLT), Good News Bible (GNB) or the Contemporary English Version (CEV). I have used all of these translations in **Essential 100**. If you are unsure about which Bible translation to use, you might want to check with a pastor, minister, priest, or Christian leader.

You will notice that each study follows a 5-step format:

Pray – Read – Reflect – Apply – Pray

In fact this is a pattern you can use any time you read the Bible. In the Bible, God speaks to you. In prayer, you can respond to him. So by integrating the two, you can actually have a conversation with God.

Here's what to do in each of the five steps:

PRAY before you read, asking God to help you understand his Word to you. The written prayer will get you started, but feel free to add whatever you'd like to express to God. Remember, you're beginning a conversation.

READ the Bible passage carefully. If you have time, you may want to read the passage more than once, or review the surrounding passages for context. Keep a pencil or highlighter handy, so you can make notes or underline key phrases or verses.

REFLECT on what you've read. Summarise your own observations on the passage in the space provided or in a notebook. It may help to ask:

- What is the main point of this passage?
- Which verses relate to my life right now?

Then read the notes commenting on the passage.

APPLY what God teaches you from his Word to your life. Take some time to think this through. Did the passage contain

- an example to follow?
- a warning to heed?
- a promise to claim?

How should this affect your thoughts, words and actions? Again, you might like to jot down how you'd like to apply these things in your life either in the space provided or in your own notebook.

PRAY again, asking God to help you live out his Word. This time, turn the things you've learned into prayers. Pray about your own needs and the needs of others. And be sure to thank God for any answers to prayer.

When you reach the end of each section you might want to use the special page to review what you've understood so far. What are the most significant insights you've gained from the five readings? Review will help you keep in mind a clear picture of what God is saying to you on your journey through the Bible

At the back of **Essential 100**, or in the back of your notebook, you might want to record a personal prayer journal. Note down both prayer requests and answers to prayer. Refer to it often so you can begin to see God at work in your life and in the lives of those around you.

Other approaches

Some people find they are better motivated to tackle a programme of Bible reading when they do it alongside others. If you're part of a church small group already, meeting regularly for fellowship, prayer or Bible study, then consider getting the whole group to commit to reading through **Essential 100.** You can compare your experiences and insights and encourage one another to keep going. Or you might want to tackle **Essential 100** within your family, with your prayer partners or within a prayer triplet.

Some groups, particularly youth groups, have used **Essential 100** as a fund-raising challenge. They have raised sponsorship from friends and family to complete the 100 readings. As a sponsored event **Essential 100** can be completed by people reading alone, by groups meeting for encouragement, or even by a group reading all 100 passages, notes and prayers aloud non-stop over a weekend. This kind of event will not only be of personal benefit to those taking part, but will raise the profile of the Bible in your church and community.

Your higher goal: meeting God

The 39 books of the Old Testament and the 27 books of the New Testament were written by many authors over a 1,500-year time span. And yet, each author was uniquely inspired by God. As the apostle Paul said, 'All Scripture is inspired by God and is useful to teach us what is true...' (2 Timothy 3:16). The apostle Peter said, 'For prophecy (the Bible) never had its origin in the will of man, but men spoke from God as they were carried along by the Holy Spirit' (2 Peter 1:21). And Jesus emphasised this truth when he quoted from Deuteronomy, 'It is written, "Man shall not live by bread alone, but by every word that proceeds from the mouth of God".'(Matthew 4:4).

What distinguishes the Bible from any other book is its divine origin. That's why people often refer to it as God's Word; it records what he's said, what he's done and what he wants from you.

So as you begin your journey through **Essential 100**, remember that your goal is not just to read the world's greatest book, or to gain more Bible knowledge, or even to develop greater spiritual discipline. All those things are important. Your higher goal is to meet the Author. The secret to making Bible reading more than just a good habit is to think of it as an opportunity to meet God – to have an encounter with the God who made you, who loves you and who desires to have a living relationship with you. If you're unsure now or at any other point that you have begun that relationship with God, you can check that out by turning to page 158.

My prayer is that over the next few months the Bible and its timeless message will come alive for you as never before. But don't let these 100 readings be the end of your journey in the Bible. Let **Essential 100** become the beginning of a lifetime adventure of meeting God daily in the Bible and prayer.

Now let's get started!

Whitney T Kuniholm

IN THE BEGINNING

If you wanted to develop a close friendship with another person, you'd want to find out as much as you can about them ... where they come from, how they grew up and what they did before you met, what interests them, what their values are.

If you wanted to buy a house, you'd investigate when it was built, what special features were part of the original design, and how the property has been maintained over the years.

But if you want to understand where the world came from, or, for that matter, where people came from, where can you go? That's where our first five readings can help. They describe the creation of the world, the birth of humankind, and the beginnings of civilisation. It makes for pretty interesting reading.

The Bible begins with arguably the most famous opening sentence ever written, 'In the beginning God...'. It makes no apology for this fundamental assertion: God exists. That's the truth upon which the entire book and all of life is based. You can read the Bible as history. Or you can read the Bible as literature. And certainly it is both. But ultimately the Bible is a book about God and that's what makes it unique.

Another feature of these five readings is that they introduce us to a number of 'firsts'. We read about the first people, the first sin, the first guilty conscience and the first case of pride. Because we're reading about the beginning of time and human history, everything is a first. But even though it all happened many years ago, the themes have a very contemporary ring.

It's worth considering one other first from these readings: God's first recorded words: 'Let there be light.' As you continue using **Essential 100**, you'll discover that God's intention has always been to bring light into the darkness. He did this in the most incredible way by sending his own son, Jesus Christ, to die on the cross and break the power of darkness once and for all.

But that's getting ahead of ourselves. There are some important things we need to learn about God, the world and ourselves first...

1

Date: _____

PRAY   Father God, please 'open my eyes to see the wonderful truths in your law' Psalm 119:18.

READ   Genesis 1,2

REFLECT

Right from the start, the Bible introduces us to its main character, 'In the beginning... God' (1:1). The rest of this unique and wonderful book is all about him. Theologians describe the Bible as God's 'self-revelation'. That means it's not only a book *about* God, it's also a book *by* God. He inspired the human writers (see 2 Peter 1:21; 2 Timothy 3:16). So if you want to meet God, read his book.

Next, the Bible tackles one of life's biggest questions: How do we explain the origins of the universe? Some scientists look in the rocks and seas for answers. But the Bible looks to the heavens (1:1). Of course, science has its place in helping us explore the natural world. But to truly explain it, we must accept that God made it, and our reading gives us two perspectives on how he did it.

The big picture (1:1–2:3) As we read this overview of the seven days of creation, we notice that God took the initiative. He had a plan and a design for his world. Experiences like holding a newborn baby or looking at the stars on a clear night are evidence of how incredible his design is.

The human interest story (2:4–25) Genesis 2:4 is like a 'hyperlink' to more information on a key part of the story – the creation of humankind. We've already learned that God chose to make men and women, and that both reflect his image (1:27). Now we learn that people possess at least two other distinctives: God's life (2:7) and God's standards (2:16,17). We have a God-given conscience, an innate sense that there is such a thing as right and wrong. To live as if it were not so is inhuman.

APPLY   What evidence for the existence of God do you see in the world around you? When do you feel closest to God?

PRAY   Thank you, Lord God, for the incredible design and beauty of your creation. Help me do a better job of caring for it.

2

Eyes wide open

Date: _____

PRAY   Lord, I'm really grateful that you've given us the Bible and that I have the freedom to read it. Help me to understand what you have to say to me today.

READ   Genesis 3

REFLECT

Popular culture sometimes portrays sex as 'the original sin'. But that's not what the Bible says. In fact, the joy of sexual intimacy between a husband and a wife is part of God's design for creation (2:23–25). Rather, the original sin was to question (3:1), challenge (3:4) and then disobey (3:6) God's definition of right and wrong (2:16,17). Both Adam and Eve made that tragic mistake and it has affected all creation ever since. We only have to read history or – if we are honest – look at our own lives to see this is true.

Sin brought immediate consequences. For Eve it meant increased pain in childbirth and a new strain in her relationship with her husband (3:16). For Adam, sin meant pain in his work and futility in his life (3:17–19). Can you imagine what it would be like if our relationships were always satisfying and our work was always meaningful?

But the biggest consequence of sin was not just that it warped God's perfect creation. It caused a breakdown in our relationship with God. Adam and Eve had enjoyed a unique and close fellowship with God (3:8,9), but now they became fearful of him and tried to hide (3:10). Compounding the problem, they began to rationalise their behaviour and we witness the introduction of guilt into the world (3:11–13). Finally, Adam and Eve were banished from God's presence with no return (3:23,24).

Pain, sorrow, futility, guilt, difficulty in relating to others, separation from God. What a horrible predicament sin has placed us in! But the Good News is that God had a plan to solve that problem.

APPLY   What makes you feel guilty? Have you done anything in the last week or so that you deeply regret? How could you make things right with others and with God?

PRAY   Lord, it's hard for me to admit it, but I have a problem with sin. Please forgive me and help me to live in a way that pleases you.

3   Clean sweep!

Date: _____

In the beginning

PRAY   Father, I've got many things on my mind and heart today. Help me to set them aside so that I can spend some quality time with you.

READ   Genesis 6:5–7:24

REFLECT

In our last reading, we saw how people decided to leave God's path and go their own way. The Bible calls that decision sin, and in our reading today we see how far from God sin will take us (6:5). It's the nature of sin that it always gets worse. It grows like cancer. Left unchecked, sin will destroy us. So we can understand why God is so upset. It's hard to let someone you love make bad choices.

Some people think that God is waiting, just waiting to catch them doing something wrong, as if he enjoys punishing people. But it's interesting that his first emotion here is not satisfaction or even anger. Rather, it's pain and grief (6:6,7). That's what our sin does to the heart of God. And, as we've learned, sin brings horrible consequences which eventually force God to act; like a potter who starts again with a lump of clay that is misshapen.

We again 'hyperlink' to the story of Noah (6:9–7:24), a man who lived in contrast to the sin and violence all around him. And why was God so pleased with Noah? Because he was willing to listen to and obey God's word (6:22; 7:5). That's the definition of righteousness. And think about the phrase, 'after the seven days' (7:10). We can only imagine how Noah felt during that week. Even so, he obeyed God when it made no sense and there were no visible results. God is still pleased today with that kind of faith.

The Flood made a clean sweep of the sin-prone culture of that day (7:22,23). But it was temporary. This was not to be the end of the world. Even as God unleashed this overwhelming judgement of sin (7:17–24), he promised a new beginning (6:18). In spite of the dark clouds, we get another hint that God has a plan for the salvation of the world.

APPLY   Do you find yourself in situations where you are surrounded by sin? How can you respond in ways that are pleasing to God?

PRAY   Lord God, I want to follow your way for my life. Please help me to keep my eyes on you and your path, no matter what those around me are doing.

4

Never again

Date: _____

PRAY   Father God, I worship and praise you. Please give me a sense of your presence as I read your Word today.

READ   Genesis 8:1–9:17

REFLECT

We used to have a beagle named Rascal. He was pretty highly strung. When I opened the door to take him for a walk, he'd go berserk with joy and bolt for the open lawn, scraping my knuckles and the leash against the door. So I can easily imagine the joyful eruption that is captured in Genesis 8:18,19. Free at last!

But were they? Yes, Noah, his family and the animals were free from that smelly ark, but were they free from the stench of sin? Had the Flood wiped that slate clean? As we will soon see in our readings through the Bible, the answer is a very definite and sad 'no'.

Noah seems to understand this underlying dilemma to life. That's why his first act was not to party; it was to worship. God is pleased when we humbly seek him (8:21,22). Noah's response to God also hints at one of the great themes in the Bible – sacrifice as a way of seeking forgiveness for sin. We'll see this throughout the Old Testament, and when we get to the New Testament, we'll discover it's the key for understanding the death and resurrection of Jesus Christ.

Of course, God understands the reality of sin all too well, but that's what makes his promise to Noah all the more poignant (9:8–17). 'Even though' God knows human beings are hopeless sinners (8:21), 'never again' will he completely destroy them (8:21; 9:11,15). In fact, he goes to great lengths to assure them that his intent was to do just the opposite. At this point in history, a rainbow would be the symbol of his love. But before long, he would come down and say it in person.

APPLY   What things most remind you that God loves you? What one thing could you do today to show God you are grateful for his love?

PRAY   Thank you, Lord, that you love me even though you know all the secrets of my heart. Help me to share your love with others today.

5   Can we talk?

Date: _____   *In the beginning*

PRAY   Help me to quiet my heart and mind, Father God, so I can hear your voice today.

READ   Genesis 11:1–9

REFLECT

What was so bad about the Tower of Babel? After all, jobs were being created, people were working together for a common purpose, technological progress was being made and society seemed to be on the verge of a lasting achievement. A track record like that would get any politician elected today. So what was the problem?

Perhaps we get a clue in Genesis 11:4. The driving motivation for all this seemingly good work was to gain *human* glory rather than God's glory. And here we confront what C S Lewis called 'the worst of all vices' – pride. Ever since the Fall, people had increasingly chosen to go their own way instead of God's. This fantastic tower became a defiant human statement: 'We're in charge here.' But it wasn't true – and that's why God confused and scattered the people of Babel (11:7–9). God won't let our unbridled pride continue forever (Proverbs 16:18).

At the same time, God affirmed the power of good communication in the most incredible way (11:6). Imagine what could be accomplished in our political arenas, our workplaces, our churches and especially our families if we were able to communicate effectively with each other while at the same time avoiding the power games of pride. Nothing would be impossible! But the sad truth is, pride is here to stay. And it's infected us all.

In the end, the tower didn't come crashing down. It was left standing on a deserted plain, a monument to the futility of trying to live without God. This story would have come to a very different conclusion if the people had followed Noah's example (8:20–22). When we acknowledge and worship God, he can accomplish incredible things through us.

APPLY   Have you got difficult or even broken communication in your family? Your church? Your place of work or study? How has pride been a factor? How could you change the situation?

PRAY   O Lord, no matter how hard I try, pride seems to sneak into my heart. Forgive me and help me to be humble in all that I do.

IN THE BEGINNING: REVIEW

From the five readings in this section, summarise any significant insights and any thoughts on applying them to your life.

1

_____

_____

_____

2

_____

_____

_____

3

_____

_____

_____

4

_____

_____

_____

5

_____

_____

_____

ABRAHAM, ISAAC AND JACOB

The Bible got off to a great start with the miracle of creation and the beauty of the Garden of Eden. But, as we've seen, once sin entered the world everything took a turn for the worse. After less than a dozen chapters in Genesis, God has already had to punish humankind by nearly wiping them out with a flood and then scattering them because of their pride at the Tower of Babel.

The world was unravelling and the biggest problem was that people couldn't do anything about it. Their only hope was for God to do something – and quick! That's why our next five readings are so important. They show us what God did, taking the first step to save us. His plan was to create a great nation – Israel – and then through them to bless the whole world with a Saviour.

His first step was to choose Abraham (or Abram as he was called when we first meet him). Abraham, his son Isaac and his grandson Jacob, are sometimes referred to as the Patriarchs. They were the first building blocks in God's great family. As you'll see, they weren't perfect. They had weaknesses: they resisted God, they sinned. But God still used them. That should be an encouragement to us. God's plan isn't thwarted by our mistakes.

We may also wonder why God did it. Why did he go to the trouble of reconciling himself to us? Why not just have another huge flood and be done with it? There can be only one answer. As C S Lewis wrote in *The Screwtape Letters*, 'He *really* loves the hairless bipeds He has created' (Letter 14).

There's one more theme you'll want to keep an eye on in these readings: faith. That's the main thing Abraham got right. He didn't know why God had picked him, he didn't know where God was sending him, and he certainly didn't know what God's plan was. All he knew was that God said 'Leave home' and so he did. Trusting God with your life is what faith is all about. In the New Testament, the apostle Paul explains that Abraham's example pointed to a bigger step of faith – believing in Jesus Christ as Saviour and Lord (Romans 4:16–25). Have you taken *that* step of faith yet?

6

Why me?

Abraham, Isaac and Jacob

PRAY Heavenly Father, your Word is such an incredible gift! Speak to me in some specific way through it today.

READ Genesis 12

REFLECT

Of all the people in the world, why did God single out Abram to receive such an incredible promise (12:2,3)? Our passage doesn't give us many clues. But it does remind us that God had a plan; he wanted to bless the whole world. Sin made it impossible for people to fix their broken relationship with God (3:23,24) and receive this blessing.

Because God took the initiative here in reaching out to Abram doesn't mean that we have no responsibility for developing a relationship with God. During his 75 years Abram had apparently cultivated the habit of listening for God's voice. Have you? He was also willing to obey. When God told him to leave home (12:1) Abram left – even when the destination was unknown. Are you willing to give up something... everything... to follow God? And Abram didn't forget about God along the way. He frequently took time out to remember what God had done and to cultivate his relationship with him (12:7,8). Have you?

The fact that Abram is one of the great examples of faith in the Bible (15:6; Romans 4:1–25) makes his reaction to the famine so curious (12:10). After all God had said and done, wouldn't you think Abram could trust God for food? Instead, Abram relocates to Egypt (note that God didn't tell him to go) and then comes up with a lame story to 'protect' himself and his wife. Even when we know what God wants us to do, we still mess it up. Thankfully, God stays with us even when we make poor choices. We may have to face tough or painful consequences. But God never leaves us. In fact, he often uses the detours of our lives to teach us things we'd never otherwise learn.

APPLY How did God find you? How have you responded to him? What detours have you encountered in your journey through life? What did God teach you through these experiences?

PRAY Thank you, Father, for making the first move to find me. I don't fully understand your love for me, but I'm so grateful for it. Help me to follow you, every step of my journey.

7

He feels your pain

Date: _____

Abraham, Isaac and Jacob

PRAY   Lord, you know the secrets of my heart. I invite you to show me the areas of my life that you want to fill and use.

READ   Genesis 15

REFLECT

It must have been a nerve-wracking time for Abram. He was already well past retirement age (12:4) when God told him to leave everything behind and head off to an unknown destination. God doesn't always give us a detailed road map in life. Often he just shows us what to do next. Faith is trusting that God will get us to the right destination. But having faith doesn't mean everything will be easy or make sense.

A sensitive issue The inability to have children was a cause for shame in ancient times, especially for women. God's amazing promise to build a nation had become the source of emotional pain for Abram and Sarai (15:2,3). 'We don't even have one child yet!' But God was using this issue of greatest sensitivity to build Abram's faith (15:6). What are you sensitive about right now? Deep down, what do you fear the most? I don't mean to trivialise the pain you feel. But sometimes the only way to deal with our fear and pain is to honestly say, 'God I hate this, and I need you to show me what you are trying to teach me.'

An impossible task Whenever we follow God's will there comes a point when things look bleak. Abram finds the land filled with '-ites' (15:19). Now what? God knows Abram needs encouragement so he gives him a peek at the master plan (15:12–21). Don't you wish he'd do that for you? 'God, if you'd just email your plan in advance that would really help.' Actually, there's a sense in which God *has* revealed his plan to us. We get the clearest picture by reflecting on what he's done in the past – in the Bible and in our lives – and then trusting that he'll be faithful in the future.

The greatest thing God does for Abram is not to build his faith or reveal his will. It is to let him experience his presence. Ultimately it is real experience of God that wipes away our fear, pain and questions, and enables us to go through anything in life with courage and joy.

APPLY   Are there any '-ites' in your life – things that seem impossible to overcome? How could you respond to these things in a way that shows your faith in God?

PRAY   Lord, you know the things in my life that cause me pain, anxiety and worry. Please show me how you are at work through those things, and give me the ability to trust you more.

8   Strange but true

Date: _____   *Abraham, Isaac and Jacob*

PRAY   Today I want to praise you, Father. You are so great, so good and loving to me. I want you to know how much I love you.

READ   Genesis 21:1–22:19

REFLECT

We begin today with a story so odd it would make headlines in the *Daily Mail:* 90-year-old woman pregnant – by 100-year-old man! But this story *is* true and demonstrates once again that God can do the impossible, not only in the pages of the Bible, but also in your life. Since our last reading, God has provided a personal reminder of his plan to build a nation by changing Abram's name, which means 'exalted father', to Abraham, which means 'father of many' (17:5). It was a reminder he would soon need.

The story gets odder still when God instructs Abraham to sacrifice his only son Isaac (22:2). Any parent will immediately feel the horror of such a dilemma. But perhaps the most amazing part of the story is that Abraham wastes no time in obeying God. 'Early the next morning... ' (22:3) he sets out. There is no arguing or questioning God's intention this time. It took a lifetime but Abraham has learned to trust God no matter what. That's still the goal of the Christian life.

What Abraham couldn't see was that God was using what seemed like a cruel test to make a profound statement. As the tension mounts in front of the makeshift altar, Abraham unwittingly prophesies God's plan of salvation: 'God himself will provide the lamb for the burnt offering' (22:8). Indeed, God did provide the lamb – his only Son Jesus Christ, who died on the cross as the once-and-for-all sacrifice for our sins. That's the 'big story' in a nutshell. The Lamb of God is at the heart of the Good News.

It's true that God sometimes tests us and it doesn't feel good when he does. But God's tests build our faith like nothing else can, and produce blessing in our lives far greater than we'll ever be able to see at the time (22:15–18). And no matter what happens, we can trust that God's plan is the best thing for us (Romans 8:28).

APPLY   Is God testing you in some way at this time? How do you think God wants to build your faith through it?

PRAY   Father, I don't fully understand your love for me, or your ways. But I want to trust you no matter what. Help me to listen for your voice and follow you throughout the journey.

9

Analyse that!

Abraham, Isaac and Jacob

PRAY   Father, thank you for inviting me to be part of your family.
Help me to live in ways that bring honour to you.

READ   Genesis 27,28

REFLECT

A psychiatrist could have a field day analysing this dysfunctional family:
a permissive father, a controlling mother, an errant older son and a decep-
tive younger son. Get them all fighting for the family inheritance and hey
presto! you've got a great plot line for any TV soap. But this is one of the
most important families in the Bible because God used them to build the
nation of Israel. So let's take a closer look at what's going on here.

In ancient times, 'the blessing' was an important way to pass on the wealth
and leadership of a family. And, from the way Isaac treated it, the blessing
seemed to have some kind of spiritual impact as well (27:27–40). The
importance of this kind of blessing is not just an ancient custom. Parental
affirmation is still one of our most basic needs as humans and whether we
receive it or not can either strengthen or weaken us for the rest of our lives.
Children today are desperate for the love and acceptance of their parents,
especially their fathers. When that's not possible, godly adults can have a
huge and positive impact by extending a blessing to the children in their
circle of influence.

But the truth is, no family is perfect. God uses broken people to accomplish his purposes. He has no other choice. Take Jacob, for example. He lets
his mother manipulate him, uses a 'trick or treat' costume to steal his
brother's blessing and then has to run for his life. But Jacob's failure iso-
lates him so that God can deal with him in a personal way (28:10–22). As
painful as they may be, the broken parts of our lives are some of the best
opportunities to have an encounter with the living God.

APPLY   What patterns – both healthy and otherwise – from your
childhood have significantly shaped you today? How could
you be a more godly influence in your family?

PRAY   Lord Jesus, I pray that you would draw my family members
closer to you. Please show me how I can be part of what
you are doing in their lives.

10   True reconciliation

Date: _____   *Abraham, Isaac and Jacob*

PRAY   Lord, thank you for accepting me. I love you and praise you today. I want to learn everything you want to teach me.

READ   Genesis 32,33

REFLECT

Sometimes guilt motivates people to do bad things – like lying or covering up the truth with a new crime. Here's an example of guilt motivating someone to do a good thing. Jacob obviously had a guilty conscience. Years earlier he had deceived his brother Esau and stolen both his birthright and blessing. Now Jacob's guilt causes him to take steps to be reconciled with his brother.

But was it really reconciliation that Jacob was after? Probably not! Jacob was just hoping to save his own skin by flattering and paying off his brother (32:13–21). Even his prayer life had a guilty ring (32:11). True reconciliation involves a change of heart first and then a change of actions. Sometimes it takes a long time for God to change our hearts, mostly because it is so difficult for us to admit our sin. But, until we do, we substitute rationalising for true reconciliation and remain trapped by our guilt and sin.

Ironically, it is Esau who exhibited true reconciliation. Years earlier, he was a driven man, bent on getting even. Now he is a contented man (33:9), who holds no grudges and is willing to genuinely embrace his nervous brother. Esau is an Old Testament example of the loving father in the parable Jesus told many years later (Luke 15:11–32). The point is, God can reconcile our most broken relationships. But we must let him do it his way; we must be willing to change.

Sometimes, life can make us so guilty, bitter or angry that the only thing that can change our hearts is a genuine experience of God. That's what happened to Jacob (32:22–32). If there are difficult relationships and situations in your life right now, maybe you need to stop asking God to change the circumstances. Instead, pray that God would help you understand and accept how he's trying to use those circumstances to change you.

APPLY   Think of a relationship in your life that is strained or broken. What might God be trying to teach you through it? In what way could you change to make things better?

PRAY   Heavenly Father, you have welcomed me with open arms. Please help me to show your all-embracing love, even to those who frustrate and irritate me.

ABRAHAM, ISAAC AND JACOB: REVIEW

From the five readings in this section, summarise any significant insights and any thoughts on applying them to your life.

1

_____

_____

_____

2

_____

_____

_____

3

_____

_____

_____

4

_____

_____

_____

5

_____

_____

_____

Before you begin each new section you may find it helpful to read through your previous Review pages as a reminder of what God has been teaching you.

THE STORY OF JOSEPH

Our next five readings will take us through the story of Joseph. As you will see, the Bible gives Joseph a lot of 'air time'. And we can reasonably ask, 'Why?' What's so important about this one man that he should get fourteen chapters in Genesis devoted to the ups and downs of his life?

For one thing, the story of Joseph forms an important bridge between the patriarchs (Abraham, Isaac and Jacob) and Moses. Most people know the story of how Moses confronted Pharaoh and commanded him to 'Let my people go'. But it's the story of Joseph that shows us how and why the people of Israel got to Egypt in the first place.

Another thing about Joseph's life is that it clearly demonstrates God's sovereignty – that is, his complete control over everything. No matter how bad the situation gets for Joseph, and it gets pretty bad, God is always using it for good (Genesis 50:20, Romans 8:28). That's an encouraging reminder when we face crisis and problems in our lives today.

Perhaps the most significant aspect of the Joseph narrative is that it becomes the next chapter in the 'big story' of the Bible, God's plan of salvation for all people. Years earlier God told Abraham that his family would become a great nation and would be a blessing to the whole world. But at this point, Abraham's descendents are a motley bunch of nomadic wanderers with a history of family problems. It looked as if a famine would break up the family and put an end to the 'big story'.

But God let Joseph and his brothers get into a jam so that he could demonstrate his willingness and ability to deliver his chosen people. At this point in the 'big story', the deliverance is from famine and oppression (Genesis 45:4 – 7). Later, God would accomplish a much greater deliverance from sin and death, through the work of his Son Jesus Christ. That was the great blessing God had in mind from the beginning and that's what makes the story of this one man so important.

11

Date: _____

Family feud

PRAY   Lord, I really enjoy having this opportunity to be close to you. Please help me to understand what I read and what you want me to do in response.

READ   Genesis 37

REFLECT

It doesn't take a genius to figure out why this family had problems. As with most sibling rivalry, it's rarely the fault of only one person. When things go wrong we tend to remember the big row, but it usually takes some time for tensions to get to boiling point. Let's take a look at what caused things to heat up in Joseph's family.

Favouritism Joseph probably was a gifted child. But that was no excuse for his father to show favouritism and rub it in with a conspicuous gift (37:3). In so doing, Jacob opened the door to a lot of bitterness. One of the most destructive things in a family is when 'love' becomes a tool for manipulation or control.

Arrogance Surely Joseph knew that no one likes a tell-tale – especially older brothers (37:2). But he doesn't seem to care. He even uses his spiritual experiences to tease his brothers (37:5–9). God has given each of us spiritual gifts. But to be used effectively, they must be combined with humility.

Jealousy What bothered the brothers most is that they wanted what Joseph had – their father's blessing (37:11). Imagine how different things might have been if Jacob had called a family meeting to say, 'I love each one of you'. Are there people in your family who need to know you love them?

Hatred Three times our passage says Joseph's brothers hated him (37:4,5,8). If we let our angry feelings go unresolved they'll destroy us from the inside out. Much better to follow Jesus' example (Matthew 5:43-48, Matthew 18:15–17) and deal with the little offences before they fester into full-blown hate.

APPLY   What causes tension and conflict in your family? How could you express genuine love to the ones who need it most?

PRAY   Father, I'm so thankful that you love me. Help me to truly love the people around me, especially those in my family.

12

Not fair!

The story of Joseph

PRAY   Lord, you have been so good to me. Thank you for the
many ways you have blessed me.

READ   Genesis 39–41

REFLECT

When we first met Joseph, he was an egotistical teenager who deliberately
irritated his family. Even though he needed to be taught a lesson this is a
pretty tough way to learn it: sold into slavery, falsely accused, thrown into
prison. How could this be God's plan?

But something happened to Joseph along the way. Maybe the trauma of
being rejected by his brothers and trapped far from home has caused some
deep reflection. Or maybe he's simply realised that his life was headed in
the wrong direction. Whatever it was, Joseph has matured. In fact, he's
become a model of moral strength (39:8–10) and sensitive to the opportunities for ministry around hlm (40:6–8).

How do you react when life is unfair? Do you lash out at the people around
you? Do you give up and give in to depression. Do you blame it on God?
Joseph had every right to do all of that and more. But he didn't, and there
are at least two reasons why.

He put God at the centre When Potiphar's wife tries to tempt him, Joseph
realises God is the one he's accountable to (39:9). And later in prison he
gives credit to God for the ability to interpret dreams (40:8b). Joseph put
God at the centre of his life and it gave him a whole new perspective and
power to deal with the problems he faced.

He trusts God's plan On the surface, Joseph's life is a mess. But under the
surface God is in control (39:2,21). Times of crisis enable us to deepen our
relationship with God. We shouldn't go looking for trouble, but tough
times do offer us some of the best opportunities to grow in our faith. But
to seize these opportunities we must trust that God has a plan – both when
things go well and when they don't.

APPLY   What tough times are you experiencing right now? Spend
some time in 'listening prayer' asking God to show you
what he wants to teach you and how you can grow closer
to him.

PRAY   Lord, I hate it when things go wrong in my life. But I really
want to grow closer to you, so please help me to see what
you are doing in the tough places.

13

The inside story

Date: _____

The story of Joseph

PRAY   Jesus, draw me closer to you as I read and reflect today.

READ   Genesis 42

REFLECT

Joseph's brothers weren't thinking about the cruel, unfair thing they had done in the desert years earlier. They were just trying to find some food for the family. But 'what goes around comes around' and Joseph realises it's payback time. Do you think he took some pleasure in accusing his brothers of being spies (42:7–17)?

But our passage is much more than a story of revenge. When we examine each of the characters, we realise there's something deeper going on. Take Joseph, for example. On the surface he appeared to be extremely successful, powerful and in control. But inside he carried a wounded soul and was longing for the love and acceptance of his family (42:22–24; 43:30).

The brothers seemed like honest, responsible family men doing their duty in a time of crisis. But inside they were consumed by guilt (42:21) and afraid that God was about to 'zap' them at any moment. And poor old Jacob looked like the wise family patriarch. But inside he had become bitter, afraid and fatalistic.

Have you ever felt the tension of trying to look good while you feel miserable? We all experience that at some point and it's one of the worst dilemmas of life. But looking good alone will never solve our problems. In fact, looking good makes it more difficult to get help. 'How can I admit the way I really feel when people think I'm such a good parent/employee/pastor/Christian? They'll never understand.' Therapy can identify our inner problems but only God through his Holy Spirit can truly resolve them. That's why the Church isn't a place for people who think they are perfect. Rather, it's a place where people who aren't afraid to admit they're broken can be healed and set free.

APPLY   What do people think about you? How are you feeling on the inside today? Are there issues you need to resolve? What steps could you take this week?

PRAY   Father God, sometimes I exhaust myself just trying to look good. Holy Spirit, please help me discover true forgiveness, love and acceptance in the deepest parts of my life.

14

Date: _____

Mind games

PRAY   You know how I'm feeling today, Lord as I come to spend time with you. Please open my heart to the things you want me to know.

READ   Genesis 43,44

REFLECT

Joseph had resisted evil in the past (39:10) but this temptation was almost too much. After all his brothers had done it must have been difficult to restrain himself. 'Throw me in a pit! Sell me down the river! Wreck my life! OK, let's see how you like a taste of your own medicine!' Joseph had the upper hand and the power to crush his helpless siblings. But he didn't – and it's worth asking why.

We don't usually think of anger as a temptation. Actually, it's not anger itself that is so bad. Getting angry is part of being human. Even Jesus got mad (John 2:12–17). But anger can tempt us to respond in the wrong way to those who offend us. 'Yes, I'm angry... but he deserved it!' But two wrongs don't make a right. That's why the Bible says, 'Be angry but do not sin' (Psalm 4:4; Ephesians 4:26).

Joseph buys some time by playing mind games with his brothers. He asks about their father, plants a silver cup in their sacks and lines them up in birth order. Some may criticise him for not letting them off the hook right away. But real life isn't like that. Some hurts are so deep they take time and gradual pressure from God to get them out in the open. If you're feeling pressure or even anger about things in your past, maybe God is trying to tell you something. One of the best responses to past anger is to pray.

But the main reason Joseph didn't blow his brothers away is that he still loved them. Often we find that underneath our angriest feelings is a deep love. That's why lashing out is the worst thing you can do when you're angry. Joseph wisely finds a private place to weep (43:30). Honestly grieving about the hurts of the past is another essential step in the healing process. God uses it to soften our hardened hearts. Eventually, Joseph and his brothers would have to forgive and reconcile. But they weren't there yet. Stay tuned.

APPLY   Are there hurts from your past still unresolved? Do you need to find a private space to grieve and pray?

PRAY   Father, I don't want to hold onto my angry feelings, but I need your help. And Lord, I know I've hurt others by what I've done. Show me how I can help them find healing too.

15

A curious whisper

Date: _____

The story of Joseph

PRAY I open my heart and my hands to you in praise. Please accept my worship and open my eyes to whatever I need to see today.

READ Genesis 45:1–46:7

REFLECT

Citizen Kane is a classic movie about a powerful and wealthy man named Charles Foster Kane. The film begins with a curious whisper, 'Rosebud!' and throughout we wonder what it means. Early in his life, Kane's father rejected him, taking the boy's favourite sled and gruffly sending him away. The rest of the movie is the story of how Kane achieved everything in life except happiness. In the final scene, we learn that the name of the favourite sled was ... Rosebud. To Charles Kane it symbolised the broken relationship with his father, a fact that haunted him his entire life.

In this passage, Joseph reveals not only his identity, but more significantly the curious whisper that has been driving him all these years. 'Is my father still living?' (45:3). That's Joseph's 'Rosebud'. We may think a broken relationship, especially with someone we've been close to, is 'no big deal'. But it can have a bigger effect than we realise if we don't let God work in us to resolve it.

But let's not forget Joseph's brothers. How did he finally reconcile with those rascals? We've seen Joseph grieving and we've seen him praying. Now we see him forgiving his cruel brothers (45:14,15). True forgiveness is the final step in healing the wounds in our past. It takes time and we must be open to God's re-shaping, but when we forgive, it miraculously empowers us to love again. It also opens our eyes to the bigger picture of what God is doing in our lives. As Joseph said, '. . . it was not you who sent me here, but God' (45:8).

Do you want healing from the hurts of your past? Would you like to be empowered to love again? Are you eager for a clearer understanding of God's will? Then make a commitment, as far as it's possible, to resolve any broken relationships in your life. It's a real joy when the curious whisper is replaced by a song of praise.

APPLY Is there a 'curious whisper' in your mind and heart today? What steps could you take to resolve the underlying issues? How will you seek God's help?

PRAY Lord Jesus, you understand better than anyone else just how I feel. Thank you for enduring the cross so that I could be forgiven.

THE STORY OF JOSEPH: REVIEW

From the five readings in this section, summarise any significant insights and any thoughts on applying them to your life.

1

_____

_____

_____

2

_____

_____

_____

3

_____

_____

_____

4

_____

_____

_____

5

_____

_____

_____

Before you begin each new section you may find it helpful to read through your previous Review pages as a reminder of what God has been teaching you.

MOSES AND THE EXODUS

Lights, camera, action… it's time for the story of Moses and the Exodus! Whenever I read this part of the Bible, I think of the classic movie *The Ten Commandments*. I'll never forget the image of Charlton Heston, who played Moses in the film: muscular, handsome, wind blowing his hair, holding the stone tablets at the top of Mount Sinai.

The life of Moses is one of the most famous and exciting parts of the Bible. Both Christians and Jews look to Moses as an example of spiritual strength and godly conviction. And because of its emphasis on liberation, this saga has given inspiration to oppressed people – especially those trapped by the evil of slavery – for centuries. The life of Moses has come to symbolise the human quest for freedom.

But there's more to the life of Moses than what we see in the movies, as you'll discover in your next five readings. For the first 40 years of his life, Moses was part of the rich and famous of Egypt. Then he blew it all by losing his temper and spent the next 40 years in 'nowheresville' living with his in-laws, tending sheep.

Moses would have died in obscurity if it wasn't for one thing: he had an encounter with God (Exodus 3:1–4:17) and that changed everything. For the last 40 years of his life Moses was a man on a mission – staring down Pharaoh, unleashing the plagues, parting the Red Sea, receiving the Ten Commandments and leading the chosen people to the brink of the Promised Land. Talk about a grand finale!

The truth is, God can use us no matter what's happened in our past, no matter how old we are and no matter how 'out of it' we may feel. All it takes is a fresh experience of the living God. After that, you'll never be the same. Haven't seen any burning bushes lately? Don't worry, one of the best ways to encounter God every day is through the Bible and prayer, and that's what you're about to do.

Now it's your turn to get into God's story!

16   'What are you doing?'

Date: _____   *Moses and the Exodus*

PRAY   It's so good just to be still with you, Father God. Help me to set aside all the distractions in my heart and mind as I come to you right now.

READ   Exodus 1,2

REFLECT

'You must have been a beautiful baby....' Or at least that's what Pharaoh's daughter seems to have thought about Moses (2:6). Blissfully nonchalant to the suffering of the child's family (1:11–14, 22), she plucks the baby from the water and so begins the life of one of the Bible's greatest heroes (Matthew 17:1–13).

The name 'Moses' sounds like the Hebrew word for 'drawn out'. The baby who was drawn out of the river by a princess would, many years later, draw the Hebrew people out of oppression and slavery. Today, our names usually don't have the same level of significance, but it's still valuable to consider our origins. What kind of family were you born into? How did your early years shape your character?

The Bible doesn't tell us much about Moses' life after his lucky break by the river. All we know is that he became part of the Egyptian elite (2:11). But inside he was an angry young man who finally took matters into his own hands in a futile attempt to save his people (2:12). In God's work, the end doesn't justify the means. That's why prayer is so important; it helps us stay in touch with God's timing and God's ways.

As Moses disappears in a cloud of dust to Midian, he might have wondered, 'God, what are you doing?' That's a question we all ask when our lives don't go the way we want. You can be sure, God does have a wonderful plan for your life and he uses every detail – even tough times – to accomplish it.

APPLY   How have the difficulties in your life prepared you to serve God better? How would you describe your mission in life?

PRAY   Dear God, open my eyes to the things you are doing in my life. I want to be all you want me to be – even if that means there are some things I need to change.

17   Encounter with God

Date: _____

Moses and the Exodus

PRAY   Father, you know how my 'to do' list is always on my
mind. Help me set everything aside so I can concentrate on
learning from you.

READ   Exodus 3:1 – 4:17

REFLECT

At this point in his life, Moses probably wasn't a good example of the
power of positive thinking. Eighty years old, plodding away in a dead-end
job, living with his in-laws… No wonder he wanted to be by himself (3:1).

God often chooses people the world overlooks (1 Samuel 16:7). David was
an unimpressive shepherd boy; Mary was an unknown Jewish girl; Peter
was a fisherman. Here, Moses was a burned-out retiree with no pension!
It's worth reflecting on the 'forgotten people' around you. If we assume
that God works only through Christian leaders, we may miss some of the
most powerful things God wants to do. The exciting thing about the
Christian life is that God can turn up when you least expect it.

What is it like to have an encounter with God? People over the centuries
have tried to 'find God' in all sorts of ways. That desire is certainly good.
But, as Moses discovered, God is already there. He's present everywhere
and he's waiting for us (Psalm 46:10a). The real question is, do we really
want to meet him, and on his terms?

Notice the progression in Moses' interaction with God. It starts with
curiosity (3:3) then moves to fear (3:6) and finally to outright rejection
(4:13). When Moses realised God's plan for him would be difficult, he
questioned if he wanted the job. If you are really searching, God doesn't
mind honest doubts and questions. But when they become a smokescreen
for rejecting God, that's another matter (4:13,14).

The most amazing thing is that God sees what we are going through (3:7)
and he wants to be with us (3:12). The God of the universe wants you to
know who he is and what he is like. And he's gone to the most extraordinary lengths to help you understand that.

APPLY   When and in what ways have you encountered God in
your life? How has it changed you?

PRAY   God, I admit that sometimes I am hesitant to come to you.
But I really want to know more of you in my life. Open my
mind, heart and will to what you want to do in me today.

18

Plagued by doubt?

Date: _____

Moses and the Exodus

PRAY   You are worthy of all my praise, Lord God. I begin this time by worshipping you from the depths of my heart.

READ   Exodus 6:28–11:10

REFLECT

Here we have one of the classic battles between good and evil in the Bible, and for that matter, in all of human history. Ten times Moses confronts Pharaoh with a plague and a message from God, 'Let my people go... ' (7:16). But Pharaoh's incredible stubbornness proves to be his undoing. Outright rejection of God isn't the only way our hearts can become hardened. It can simply be the result of gradually doing things our own way over a period of time. In the end, the result is the same: a broken relationship with God.

Why did God bother with the ten plagues? After all, he could have saved the ecosystem and gone straight to number ten. Or he could have caused Pharaoh to keel over and given power to a more tolerant successor. The answer really has two parts. The first part is very broad: God wanted to proclaim his name, to let people know that he was the Lord (9:16; 10:2). He wants everybody in the whole world for all time to know he is God. And that he is powerful. And that he is worthy of our worship.

The second part of the answer is very personal: God also works in the lives of individuals, shaping and preparing them for the work he has called them to do. Consider Moses: he wasted the best years of his life and when God tried to give him a second chance he resisted and rejected God's plan. Moses needed one of those badges for his robe, 'Be patient... God isn't finished with me yet'. The ten plagues were not just for Pharaoh. It seems that Moses needed convincing that God alone was the Lord.

If you want to know God, the starting place is to believe that he is the Lord over the entire world. But to really know him you must make him the Lord of *your* life as well. That's what being a follower of Jesus is all about.

APPLY   What did it/will it take to convince you that God is Lord over the whole world? And over your life as well?

PRAY   Lord Jesus, help me to be your willing, trusting and faithful follower today.

19

Date: _____

Spare me!

PRAY   I praise you, Lord Jesus, that you are the Way, the Truth and the Life (John 14:6). Help me draw closer to you as I read and reflect on your life-giving Word.

READ   Exodus 12:1–42

REFLECT

Have you ever wondered what the Passover is all about? Most calendars list it, and Jewish people the world over still celebrate it. But as you read these verses, perhaps you wonder what God was thinking about! Why the elaborate instructions about the lamb and sharing, about how fast to eat the meal, and especially about what to do with the blood (12:1–11)? Our passage gives us two big hints.

God's first purpose for the Passover was *judgement* (12:12). Not only were the Egyptians cruelly forcing the Jews to be their slaves, they were also deeply involved in idolatry. God can't stand it when we participate in oppressing other people or when we worship anything other than him. The Egyptians were doing both and God had to put a stop to it with a very severe punishment (12:29,30). Today, the way we oppress people may not be with a whip; it may be economic or social. And our idolatry may not involve carved statues; it may be as simple as how we look, or our attitude to our favourite sports team. The point is, we are on dangerous ground when we suppress people or when we let things become more important to us than God.

God's second purpose for the Passover was to create a *reminder* (12:14). He wanted his people to remember how he set them free. But there was more to it than that. The lamb and the blood were symbols of a much greater salvation to come. Jesus was 'the Lamb of God' who shed his own blood to take away the sins of the world (John 1:29). In fact, Jesus specifically applied all the imagery of the Passover to himself in the Last Supper (Matthew 26:17-30). This was God's strategy for saving people from sin.

Pharaoh thought he could resist God or manipulate things to go his way. But as this passage shows us, God is in charge and he is at work accomplishing his purposes in the world. The best response is to do what the Israelites did: obey God immediately (12:28).

APPLY   Is there anything in your life that has a stronger hold on you than God? What would it take to put God at the centre of your life?

PRAY   Lord God, I know you are the one in charge of this world and of my life. Set me free of everything that holds me back from worshipping you with my whole heart.

20

The defining moment

Date: _____

PRAY   'Your Word is a lamp to my feet and a light for my path'
(Psalm 119:105). May that be true today, Lord.

READ   Exodus 13:17–14:31

REFLECT

Some people think that the crossing of the Red Sea was the defining
moment for Moses. It certainly must have been spectacular to see all that
water piled up in a great wall. And who's going to challenge a leader who
can do something like that? 'Whatever you say, Boss!'

But our passage reveals a more powerful defining moment for Moses and
it comes just prior to parting the sea. Imagine how Moses felt. He's pinned
against the water, the most powerful army in the world is bearing down
on him with a score to settle and his own people are on the verge of a
mutiny (14:11,12). Moses may have felt like he'd made a big mistake that
was going to cause a huge disaster.

Have you ever felt that way when you've tried to do something for God?
Perhaps you've taken a leadership position in the church or community
and the whole thing comes apart with everyone blaming you? Some
people get bitter or give up. But disasters, although painful, give us the best
opportunity to grow; they force our faith to a higher level.

Instead of rationalising or running, Moses stood up and boldly proclaimed
his trust in God (14:13,14). This is one of the best examples of Christian
leadership in the entire Bible. What God had been teaching Moses through
the progression of plagues – that he was powerful, that he had a plan and
that he wants us to trust and obey – he now puts into action. It's one thing
to know all the right answers. It's another to publicly take action when the
pressure is on. But when we do that, we have a defining moment in our
own relationship with God.

APPLY   What have been the defining moments in your walk with
God? Have any of them involved pressure or even disaster?
Is there a situation in your life right now that gives you an
opportunity to boldly trust God? What would this look
like?

PRAY   Heavenly Father, you know I'd rather avoid problems. Help
me to know whether the pressures I face are the result of
my bad judgement – or your desire to stretch my faith in
you.

39

MOSES AND THE EXODUS: REVIEW

From the five readings in this section, summarise any significant insights and any thoughts on applying them to your life.

1

_____

_____

_____

2

_____

_____

_____

3

_____

_____

_____

4

_____

_____

_____

5

_____

_____

_____

Before you begin each new section you may find it helpful to read through your previous Review pages as a reminder of what God has been teaching you.

THE LAW AND THE LAND

Now that the Israelites have broken free of their bondage in Egypt, their main objective is to find a home. Land has always been important to the Jewish people, not only because they've wanted a place to call their own, but also because God had promised it to them. It's that quest to reach the Promised Land that animates our next five readings.

Sometimes people say, 'The journey is more important than the destination'. Perhaps there's a bit of truth in that for the children of Israel, because God does some incredible things while they wander in the desert. We've already seen how he parted the Red Sea and destroyed the Egyptian army. Now we'll see God thundering on Mount Sinai and giving the Ten Commandments. He'll also part the Jordan River and give the Israelites a tremendous military victory at Jericho. As they enter the Promised Land, the Israelites have momentum on their side.

There's an important theme running through these readings that you'll want to be looking for. Any success that Israel had was not due to their large army, effective strategies or good luck. It was the result of their willingness to listen to and obey God. Simple as that. It took Moses many years to learn that lesson, but once he finally got it, God really used him. Joshua had the advantage of watching Moses, so he learned the lesson faster. But you'll see that cultivating a willingness and ability to hear the Word of God and put it into action is the key to growth and effectiveness in the Christian life.

Our readings do give us a hint of dark clouds on the horizon for the chosen people. The golden calf was Israel's first direct experience with idolatry. For the rest of the Old Testament, they struggled with this destructive tendency. In the end, it alienated them from God and brought a terrible punishment. But it also highlighted their need for a Messiah, a Saviour, and that's what the New Testament is all about.

21

Date: _____

The Law and the land

PRAY   Thank you for making it clear in your Word how you want me to live. Help me to read and understand with my heart today.

READ   Exodus 19:1–20:21

REFLECT

People like to argue about the Ten Commandments. How relevant are they today? Can life really be that black and white? Isn't it just too simplistic?

But in all the arguments, most people miss the most important point. The Ten Commandments are not just a list of 'Thou shalts' and 'Thou shalt nots'. Perhaps that's the kind of prescribed religion many people want. But God isn't trying to start a religion; he's trying to build a relationship with his people (19:4–6).

It may help you to divide the commandments into three groups. The first four centre on *our relationship with God*. There's only one God (20:3) and he warns us to accept no substitutes (20:4–6). We mustn't be too casual, or worse, in referring to him (20:7). And we must regularly honour and worship him (20:8–11). Since he is the Sovereign Creator of all things, can we do any less?

Next, he cares about *our relationship with others*. Before we can 'love everybody', we need to start with the ones closest to us: our parents (20:12) and spouses (20:14). The patterns we develop here will affect all our other relationships. Our next challenge is to be truthful with our neighbours (20:16) – easier said than done in a world of manipulation and compromise. That's why it's a relief to have at least one 'easy' commandment (20:13). Except that Jesus didn't think it was so easy (Matthew 5:21,22).

Finally, God cares about *our relationship to things*. A willingness to steal (20:15) begins when we aren't content with what we have (20:17). The desire for more is a strong motivator that can pull us away from God (1 Timothy 6:6–10). If more people had a right relationship with God, others and things, the world really would be a different place. No wonder people would rather argue about the Ten Commandments than simply obey them.

APPLY   What are the things that improve or erode your relationship with God? Which of these commandments would you like to work on this week?

PRAY   Lord, I really want to know you better. Please help me care about the things that are important to you. And thank you that you love and forgive me when I fail.

22

Up close and personal

Date: _____

The Law and the land

PRAY 'Search me, O God, and know my heart; test me and know my anxious thoughts. See if there is any offensive way in me, and lead me in the way everlasting.'
(Psalm 139:23,24)

READ Exodus 32–34

REFLECT

In this passage Aaron delivers one of the funniest lines in the Bible (32:24). Talk about lame excuses! Put him in charge for just a few days and he lets the people run wild.

But before we laugh too hard at Aaron, we need to look at ourselves. With all we know about God, and after all he's done for us, how quickly we turn our backs on him to binge on wrong thoughts and actions. Even Paul struggled with this tendency (Romans 7:15–20). Being a Christian doesn't exempt us from temptation and sin. But – through Jesus – God has given us the only way to break its power over our lives (1 John 1:9).

This passage also gives us a glimpse of God's angry side (32:9,10); he really hates sin, a reality we shouldn't take lightly. Moses did too (32:19,20) and he's willing to stand in the gap to do whatever it takes to save his people (32:11–14, 31,32). In so doing, he provides a hint of what Jesus would do many years later.

But perhaps the most amazing part of this passage is the interaction between God and Moses. They developed a very personal relationship (33:11). That's what God really wants with you and me and everyone. He has no interest in a world of religious clones. He created men and women in his own image with the capacity to respond to him each in their own way, and he simply wants them to acknowledge that he is Lord by loving and following him with their whole hearts and using their own unique gifts.

APPLY How would you describe your relationship with God at this time? What things pull you away from God? What things draw you closer?

PRAY O God, we both know how quickly I give in to sin. Please forgive me, and help me to draw closer to you today.

23   **Learn it and live it**

Date: _____

PRAY   As I meditate on your Word today, guide my heart to the message you want me to hear and apply.

READ   Joshua 1

REFLECT

New pastors or ministers often struggle when they have to follow someone who was in the post a long time and was greatly loved. People can't help comparing the new leader to the old one, usually unfavourably. It can be a difficult time for both the new pastor and the congregation. So imagine how Joshua felt at this point in his 'career'. How could he get anywhere near Moses?

But a quick look back reveals that God had been preparing Joshua for this leadership challenge. Joshua had witnessed Moses leading the Israelites (Exodus 32:17), plus he had seen from Moses how to develop a real relationship with God (Exodus 33:11b). One of the best ways to grow in our spiritual lives is to find a mentor – someone older and wiser in the faith. If you want to learn it, watch someone who's living it. And if you've been a Christian for some time, pray that God will lead you to those he wants you to coach on his behalf. It's an important ministry.

God made a special effort to encourage Joshua for the task. He promised to give him land, success and a leadership platform like he gave Moses (1:3–6). Best of all, God promised to be with Joshua (1:5). Some day you may be called to serve God in a difficult situation, one that stretches you beyond your abilities. But if God has called you to a task, he will be with you. Difficult situations can be an opportunity to experience God.

In return for all these promises and help, God asked only one thing from Joshua: obedience (1:7). It sounds so easy, but it's not – mostly because we're sinful. That's why God gave Joshua his Word and instructed him to really soak it in (1:8). If you want to live an effective Christian life the secret is reflecting on God's Word (meditating) and applying what it says (doing). That's why right now is potentially the most important part of your day.

APPLY   Which challenge fits you best at this time: to find a spiritual mentor or be a spiritual mentor? Why and how will you do that?

PRAY   Father, thank you for the people who have influenced me to follow you. Please help me to keep growing and show me how I can help others grow too.

24   **Effective Christian leadership**

Date: _____   *The Law and the land*

PRAY   'Oh, how I love your law! I meditate on it all day long'
(Psalm 119:97). May this be my experience as I come to
your Word today.

READ   Joshua 3,4

REFLECT

When Joshua led the people through the Jordan River it was an exact replay
of the time Moses led the people through the Red Sea – only this time Israel's
enemies had learned not to give chase! God was using the similarities
between the two events to strengthen Joshua's leadership position (3:7).

But Joshua's success was the result of much more than his past association
with a spiritual celebrity. He had cultivated the habit of listening to God
(1:7) and obeying right away (1:9–13). That's the key to effective Christian
leadership: following orders from God. In addition, Joshua had two other
traits that made him effective in God's work. The first was *bold faith*; he
publicly announced his belief in God's power (3:5). The second was *humility*. God himself had announced his confidence in him as Moses' successor (3:7), but he didn't let it go to his head. No matter what God asks you
to do, these are the qualities that will make you successful.

Our passage also presents us with some interesting symbols. The *Ark of the
Covenant* symbolised God's presence with the people of Israel. The *Jordan
River* symbolises the death experience for many – the end of the journey
and the beginning of the Promised Land. And the *stones* from the middle
of the river were to be a sign of what God had done for his people.

What are the symbols in your Christian life? You may want to go back,
even if just in your imagination, to the significant times in your walk with
God. Is there a symbol you could use to remind you of a lesson God taught
you? Be careful not to focus so much on the symbol that you forget its
meaning. That can even happen with our Bibles. It's no use being a Bible
buff if you've lost your passion for God! Entering the Promised Land was
a spiritual high point for Israel. Unfortunately, over time, they forgot the
God who got them there.

APPLY   Which is the bigger need in your life now: greater
knowledge of God's Word or greater passion for God? How
could you begin to meet that need?

PRAY   Lord Jesus, thank you for the times in my life when you've
met me in a special way. Keep me hungry for your Word
and passionate to know you better.

25

I did it my way?

Date: _____

PRAY   Lord, I praise you for being such a great and loving God.
Thank you for the many blessings in my life.

READ   Joshua 5:13–6:27

REFLECT

If you ever went to Sunday School or a kids' club at church, you'll have enjoyed the story about how the walls of Jericho came a-tumbling down. Crash! God wanted the Promised Land free of all those who worshipped idols and free of the detestable practices that went with it. The sad part was, although the Israelites got off to this spectacular start, they never finished the job and it proved to be their undoing.

But this passage raises an uncomfortable question: wasn't God a little extreme? Wouldn't it have been better for him to let everyone worship in his or her own way? The hard fact is that God is the Creator and Lord of all. That's the message he's been communicating throughout Israel's history. To set our own conditions on God is not worship; it's rejection. The clay doesn't tell the potter what to make (Isaiah 45:9).

That doesn't mean God is intolerant. Consider what happened to Rahab. She was a non-Jew and a prostitute living in a city marked for destruction. The Bible doesn't condone her sin. But it does show that those who turn to God and demonstrate it by their actions (Joshua 2) will be saved. That's not intolerance; that's God's free gift of forgiveness and all-embracing love. Those who insist on going their own way run the risk of forfeiting that gift.

Imagine how you would have felt marching around the city. No doubt the Israelites had to endure some putdowns and catcalls from the guards on the wall. But God's ways are not our ways and once again we are reminded of the need to listen and obey God. That's a lesson God really wants to teach you because it's the key to growth and effectiveness in the Christian life.

APPLY   Is there any 'unfinished business' in your life that is
hampering your relationship with God? What is it and
how could you begin to deal with it this week?

PRAY   Father, I don't claim to understand everything about you.
But I do believe you are the Lord and I want to follow you.

THE LAW AND THE LAND: REVIEW

From the five readings in this section, summarise any significant insights and any thoughts on applying them to your life.

1

_____

_____

_____

2

_____

_____

_____

3

_____

_____

_____

4

_____

_____

_____

5

_____

_____

_____

Before you begin each new section you may find it helpful to read through your previous Review pages as a reminder of what God has been teaching you.

THE JUDGES

The Book of Judges is a part of the Old Testament that's often overlooked. Genesis and Exodus were new and exciting. The miracle of creation was followed by the adventures of Abraham, Isaac, Jacob, Joseph, Moses and Joshua. And just ahead are the books of 1 and 2 Samuel and 1 and 2 Kings, where we meet two of Israel's greatest kings, David and Solomon.

But hold on, we missed something! What happened to God's people between the time of the Patriarchs and the time of the Kings? That's what the Book of Judges is all about. The people of Israel are in the Promised Land and they've begun to grow and expand into a great nation. The problem – at least from their point of view – is that they don't have a king. The problem – from God's point of view – is that they keep turning away from him to worship idols. Why would they want to worship the Caananite fertility gods (Baal and the Ashtoreths) instead of the one true God who brought them out of Egypt with so many demonstrations of his love and power? For that matter, why do people turn their backs on God today? That's one of the underlying questions for you to ponder in these next five readings.

Because of their idolatry, God punished his people by allowing the surrounding peoples (Midianites and Philistines) to attack and oppress them for long periods of time. You can almost hear God saying, 'How many times do we have to go through this before you'll learn?' But even so, when the people finally come to their senses and cry out to God, he gives them special leaders (Judges) to save Israel from the consequences of their sin. Yet, after a few years, they forget God and start the process all over again.

The Book of Judges isn't all gloom and doom, though. It contains the stories of some of the most intriguing characters in the Bible – Deborah, Gideon and Samson. And our readings finish with one of the most romantic stories in the Bible, the Book of Ruth.

Sometimes the parts of the Bible that are the least familiar to us give us the greatest insights. That's because we bring no preconceptions; we are able to take a fresh look at what God is saying. Be prepared for something special!

26

Endangered species

Date: _____

PRAY   Heavenly Father, I long to hear your voice. Help me to
             truly listen to what you have to say to me now.

READ   Judges 2:6–3:6

REFLECT

Have you ever heard someone say, 'Christianity is dead, on the brink of
extinction'. That can be unnerving. But in fact, Christianity is *always* one
generation away from extinction! Unless Jesus' followers communicate
the reality of the gospel and the truth of God's Word, the next generation
will never know.

We certainly see an example of that in our reading today. Joshua and the
leaders around him had died (2:7), taking the stories of God's great work
with them to the grave. No matter how old you are right now, you have
an important mission for the rest of your life: to tell others – especially
younger people – what God has done for you.

Unfortunately, the Israelites failed to do that and it began a depressing
cycle in their history (2:10–19). They turned away from God, worshipped
idols and experienced disaster. Then, in desperation they cried out to God,
and he raised up leaders (Judges) and saved them. But before too long, the
cycle begins again. And again, and again.

Have you ever experienced that cycle in your life? Turning our back on
God or just gradually taking little steps away from him can lead to some
painful consequences. But even then, God is at work. Note that he planned
to use the disasters to test his people (2:22), to find out if they would really
turn to him when the chips were down. If there's anything good about
falling away from God, it's that our relationship with him is much stronger
when we return (James 1:2–4).

APPLY   Where are you in your relationship with God right now?
              Becoming a little distant? Running into trouble, or even
              disaster? What can you learn from your past that will draw
              you closer to God in the present?

PRAY   Lord God, I'm grateful that even when I falter you want to
              help me grow closer to you. Help me to remove any
              barriers to growing intimacy with you.

27

Date: _____

Girl power

PRAY   Holy Spirit, I invite you to be with me. Please give me a
           sharp mind and a tender heart as I read your Word today.

READ   Judges 4,5

REFLECT

If you're looking for a passage in the Bible that will make women and girls
feel powerful, you've found it! Deborah broke through the glass ceiling in
Israel; she's the only female judge listed in the Bible. And the hero of this
story is Jael, a young woman who had the brains and the guts to take out
the military commander Sisera. Go, girl!

But to really hear what this passage has to say, we must look deeper than
the 'boys against girls' theme. First, notice the source of Deborah's leadership. She doesn't try to take charge and she's not interested in being
upfront (4:9,10). She simply says and does what God tells her (4:6,7,14),
and it has a powerful effect.

As we saw in the life of Joshua, a spiritual leader is someone who follows
orders from God. If that's true, the path to Christian leadership is not
about attaining a prominent position or lording it over a big staff. It's
about developing the ability to listen to God. And whether you are a man
or woman, a boy or girl, you can be that kind of leader (Joel 2:28,29). In
fact, the Church desperately needs people who know how to hear and
follow God's direction.

A second theme in this passage has to do with courage, another quality
that isn't limited by gender. No one could have imagined what Heber's
hospitable wife had in mind when she invited Sisera into the tent
(4:17–21). She didn't learn *that* at the WI! But God used Jael's bold act to
defeat the powerful Caananites. The point is, we can't limit God from
using whoever he wants to do his work. Because in the end, it's our ability
to listen to God and willingness to rely on his power that makes the difference.

APPLY   How have you/could you cultivate the ability to hear and
            follow God's direction? In what area of your life do you
            most need to rely on God's power?

PRAY   Father, open my eyes to see all the people you want to use
            to do your work. With your help, I intend to be one of
            them.

28

How can I be sure?

Date: _____

PRAY　　　'I wait for the Lord, my soul waits, and in his word I put my hope. My soul waits for the Lord more than the watchmen wait for the morning, more than the watchmen wait for the morning' (Psalm 130:5,6).

READ　　　Judges 6,7

REFLECT

The very first word in this passage tells us everything we need to know about the spiritual state of Israel: 'Again... ' (6:1). How many disasters will it take for the chosen people to learn to obey God? Aaron had no idea what his compromise in the desert would lead to (Exodus 32:1–6). But that's how sin works; it doesn't seem like a big deal at first, but left unchecked it grows more and more destructive. The only way to stop it is to repent, and the sooner the better.

Enter Gideon, a man not really interested in being a leader (6:11–15). But God saw his potential (6:12) and used this difficult time in Israel's history to prepare him for a bigger challenge ahead. That should be an encouragement if you're in a frustrating situation right now. Perhaps God is preparing you for your next assignment on his behalf. What do you need to learn now?

Some question whether Gideon's request for 'signs' reveals a lack of faith (6:17–40). Can we ask for a sign today? Not if we make it some kind of magic formula. But if we genuinely seek God in faith, we can ask him to make his will clear to us. Real power and conviction come when we prayerfully wait for confirmation from God. That's what happened to Gideon.

But Gideon's success was the result of two other things: he was empowered by the Spirit (6:34) and he was forced to rely on that power (7:2). That was the whole point of reducing the army from 32,000 to 300 men. Don't be discouraged if you feel you don't have enough resources to do God's work. All he needs is one person who's willing to listen and obey.

APPLY　　　How do you listen to God? What has he been telling you? Is there a particular need or issue about which you need to wait on God for confirmation?

PRAY　　　Sovereign Lord, it's so encouraging to read about what you can do through those who trust and obey you. Please show me how to let more of your power work through me.

29

A lady's man

Date: _____

The judges

PRAY   Lord, as I prepare myself to meet you today, show me the things that are blocking my relationship with you so that I can ask for forgiveness.

READ   Judges 13–16

REFLECT

What in the world happened between chapters 13 and 14? Manoah and his wife (we never learn her name) seem like the model of godly parenting (13:8,12). They know their miracle child had been specially chosen (13:5) and empowered by God (13:25) for a great work in Israel. But somehow, Samson developed a fatal character flaw; he had no self-control and it proved to be his undoing.

Christian parents who have wayward children need special support and prayer. It can be incredibly painful to watch the ones we love make destructive choices. But we can take encouragement knowing that sometimes God is at work in ways that aren't so obvious (14:4).

Samson's lack of self-control expressed itself in two ways: lust and anger. His thoughtless pursuit of women seems comical, but it produced a string of broken relationships and violence. Not so funny. Finding a wife or husband who shares your commitment to Christ, and having the determination to work through the ups and downs of a lifelong relationship is hard work. But it's the only way to find the love and satisfaction Samson never found.

In the end, Samson becomes the classic example of a talented but flawed leader. Maybe Delilah's performance fooled him, or maybe he just gave up. But the real tragedy of Samson's life is that deep down he knew he had been running from God all along (16:17). The greatest victory in Samson's life was not his temple-crashing defeat of the Philistines. It was the fact that in his brokenness he finally turned back to God (16:28).

APPLY   What are the motivating factors in your relationships with those of the opposite sex? How could you develop relationships that honour God (1 Timothy 5:1,2)?

PRAY   Lord God, thank you for the people who are closest to me in life. Enable me to be a godly example and encouragement to them this week.

30

Love story

Date: _____

PRAY Lord Jesus, you gave up everything to die on the cross for my sin. I don't understand why you love me so much, but I'm very grateful.

READ Ruth 1–4

REFLECT

What a great love story! There's tragedy, intrigue, romance and even a happy ending. The story of Ruth is a bright spot in the depressing sin cycle we've seen in the Book of Judges. But this is much more than a romantic novel. Ruth is a tremendous example of godly character (3:11) and that's what makes this short book so helpful to us today.

Ruth's life got off to a traditional start. For ten years she was married and surrounded by her extended family (1:1–5). But when both her husband and father-in-law die, Ruth's world comes apart. Tough times often reveal our true character. We can become resentful like Naomi (1:20,21). Or we can let God use the detours in our lives to make us stronger and more like him. No matter what happens, that's the choice we must make.

So what did the tough times reveal about Ruth's character? She was *loyal*; she didn't abandon her family even though it was in her best interest to do so (1:14). She was *optimistic*; she didn't become bitter like her mother-in-law (1:13). She was a *hard worker* (2:7); she didn't give up on life because something bad had happened to her. She was *submissive*; she gracefully worked within the customs of her day (3:5,6). She had *integrity*; she didn't resort to sinful shortcuts in building a relationship with her future husband (3:7–14). And finally, she had *faith*; she committed her life to God no matter where it took her (1:16).

Today, many people try to achieve success by having a lot materially, or knowing the right people or even just looking the part. But Ruth's way was to cultivate a noble character and then trust God to bless her as he saw fit. And he certainly did that. God gave Ruth a happy marriage to a prominent man, wealth and security, and, best of all, he gave her a son who became the grandfather of King David and an ancestor of Jesus Christ (Matthew 1:5,6). Not bad for a former homeless widow.

APPLY What tough times are you facing at the moment? How might God be trying to build your character through them?

PRAY Father, I need your help to face the problems in my life. Most of all, I need you to help me become the person you want me to be through them.

THE JUDGES: REVIEW

From the five readings in this section, summarise any significant insights and any thoughts on applying them to your life.

1

2

3

4

5

Before you begin each new section you may find it helpful to read through your previous Review pages as a reminder of what God has been teaching you.

THE RISE OF ISRAEL

Who would lead the people of Israel now that they had settled in the Promised Land? That's the big question being worked out in our next five readings. As we've seen, God's plan was to form Abraham's descendants into a 'great nation' and through them to bring 'great blessing' to all people (Genesis 12:2,3). That blessing would be a Saviour for the sins of the entire world – Jesus Christ.

Because of their unique place in his plan, the Israelites experienced God's direct help and guidance over the years. It was God who freed the children of Israel from captivity in Egypt; God who led them through the desert with pillars of cloud and fire; God who brought them to the Promised Land. And along the way it was God who took the initiative to reveal his priorities by giving them the Law at Mount Sinai. Since the very beginning, God had been powerfully and miraculously leading his people.

But, as we will see, the Israelites became uncomfortable with God's leadership style; he absolutely refused to let them worship other gods or participate in all the things that went with it. Instead, they wanted a king 'like all the other nations' (1 Samuel 8:19,20). On the surface this didn't seem such an outrageous request. But behind Israel's desire for a 'normal king' was a rejection of God's rule over them (1 Samuel 8:6,7). It's the same choice we face today: to follow Jesus and be part of God's kingdom or to go our own way. It's a decision with eternal consequences.

In spite of their subtle rejection of him, God doesn't abandon his people. He gives them the kings they want and continues working out his plan through them. As a result, we are introduced to some of the Bible's greatest characters. We meet Samuel, the boy who listened to God; Saul, Israel's talented first king who came to a tragic end; and David, Israel's greatest king and 'a man after God's own heart'.

Our readings bring us to the pinnacle of Israel's history – the one time when they had both the land and peace. As we know from reading the rest of the Bible and our daily newspapers, it didn't last. But what a glorious time it was!

31

Date: _____

The real world

PRAY   Lord, I know I'm not perfect, but I'm committed to becoming the person you want me to be. I'm open to whatever you want to say to me from your Word today.

READ   1 Samuel 1–3

REFLECT

One of the things that gives the Bible the ring of truth is that it records real stories of real people. Although the events in this reading took place thousands of years ago, they could be happening today. Let's take a closer look and see what lessons we can apply to our lives today.

The stressed wife As we've seen in earlier readings (Genesis 16:1–10; 18:11,12), the inability to have children was a source of shame in ancient Israel. For Hannah, it was the cause of deep stress and personal trauma (1:8,15). How do *you* react when things in your personal life don't work out as you'd like? In spite of her pain, Hannah candidly poured her heart out to God and asked for his help (1:10–17). That's what real prayer is all about.

The overly-tolerant father For all his good qualities, Eli failed to discipline his sons when they were young and soon they were out of control (2:12–25). Today, many parents think the loving thing to do is let teenagers 'make their own decisions'. But setting appropriate limits for our children is one of the most important responsibilities of parents. That's real love.

The faithful child Several times in this reading, Hophni and Phinehas are contrasted with Samuel. What was the key difference? Samuel was willing to listen to God (3:10) while the older boys were not (2:17). The most important task of Christian parents is to model for their children how to listen to and follow God wholeheartedly. That's the ultimate reality check.

APPLY   Which character from our reading do you identify with? What do you learn from their experience that can help you? How could you do a better job of modelling your commitment to Christ to those around you – especially young people?

PRAY   Father, I need your help to demonstrate my love for you to others. Help me become an effective witness for you.

32

Date: _____

The rise of Israel

PRAY   Lord, thank you for the freedom I have to read your Word. I ask for the gift of your presence as I listen to what you want to say to me today.

READ   1 Samuel 8–10

REFLECT

It doesn't seem such a big deal that a developing nation would want its own king. After all, who's going to run the government, spend the taxes or command the army (8:10–18)? Somebody's got to be the boss.

But underneath Israel's 'reasonable' desire for a king was a rebellious motivation. They wanted to be like everyone else (8:20). After all God had done for Israel, they still wanted to go their own way (8:6–9)! That's a temptation every Christian faces. If we aren't careful, the pressure to conform, to fit in, to be accepted, can gradually lead us away from God. Jesus simply said, 'Follow me' (Mark 1:16–18). It sounds easy, but what he is really asking is to be the 'king' of your life. That's what it means to say, 'Jesus is Lord'.

Even so, Saul seemed like a good choice for Israel's 'first' king; he was tall, impressive, humble and even religious. Sometimes God gives us what we ask for – even though it's not his plan A. It may lead us down a road of greater difficulty, as it did for the Israelites. But God loves us so much that he's willing to use even the bad decisions we make to teach us some important lessons.

In Saul's case, God was also willing to give him a vital characteristic of an effective Christian leader – a heart open to the leading of the Spirit (10:5–10). That's a quality worth cultivating whether you are a leader or not, because it's how God can use you to make a difference in the lives of the people around you. Notice that being led by the Spirit is like the two sides of a coin – God must work in your heart but you must develop the ability to hear him. You can do that by reading the Bible, praying and by using your gifts (1 Corinthians 12) for the benefit of other Christians. But, like any other ability, if you don't use it you'll lose it.

APPLY   When you say, 'Jesus is Lord' what do you mean? What could you do this week to cultivate the ability to hear God better?

PRAY   Lord Jesus, I want to be a fully committed follower. Please prepare my heart so that you can use me to do your will.

33   Only a boy named David

Date: _____

The rise of Israel

PRAY Father, open my eyes to something new in your Word and my heart to your love as I seek you today.

READ 1 Samuel 16:1–18:16

REFLECT

Our passage today contains a Bible story that has become part of our culture. When a lone citizen challenges the city council, when a start-up business competes with a large corporation, when an underdog team plays the world champions – it's often likened to David taking on Goliath. But what really was the key to David's success?

First of all, it took guts for a teenager to volunteer to fight such a huge warrior (17:32). No doubt David's brothers thought his victory was due to a lucky shot. But the real reason David killed Goliath had little to do with his guts or luck. It was God's doing.

Notice that God had chosen David (16:12), filled him with his Spirit (16:13) and stayed with him all the way (18:14). God expects us to use the talents and abilities he has given us to do his work, but we must remember that the final results depend on him. That's why success and humility must go hand in hand. Ultimately David won because he understood Goliath was picking a fight with God (17:45).

That's not to say David was perfect. Grouchy old Eliab thought David was conceited and wicked (17:28). Perhaps he was at times; there's often a grain of truth in every criticism. But the Bible makes clear that David had developed an instinct for depending on God in other stressful situations (17:34–37), so when the pressure was on with Goliath, he was ready.

David's greatest strength was his heart for God (Acts 13:22). It's natural to be attracted to people who have all the right stuff – beauty, intelligence, athletic ability, charm, fame, wealth … whatever. But God makes it clear he's looking for something deeper than that (16:7). He's looking for people with hearts that are totally committed to him.

APPLY How have you reacted to the successes in your life? Who around you has a heart for God and how can you tell? How could you cultivate a heart for God?

PRAY Lord God, forgive me for comparing myself to others on superficial things. Please help me develop a heart that is eager to know and follow you.

34   First impulse

Date: _____   *The rise of Israel*

PRAY   God, how wonderful it is to be with you. I want to set aside all the distractions in my mind and heart so that I can focus on what you want to say to me today.

READ   1 Samuel 23:7–24:22

REFLECT

For me, Saul has always been one of the most tragic figures in the Bible. He started out so well: talented, humble, chosen by God and filled with the Spirit. Potentially, a surefire success. But in today's reading, Saul has become jealous, paranoid and sinful. He knew his days were numbered (23:17). What went wrong?

For all his positive traits, Saul had an impulse for doing things his own way instead of God's (13:1–15; 15:11). That's a good description of sin. Over time, that impulse warped his relationships (23:21–23), ruined his judgement (chapter 28), and led to his destruction (chapter 31). Is your first impulse in every situation to obey God? It's worth spending some time in prayerful reflection on that point, so you'll be ready when the moment of truth comes.

Imagine how different things would have been if he had repented and recommitted himself to obeying God. No matter what we've done, no matter how much we've disobeyed God, he is always willing to give us a fresh start (1 John 1:9). That's the essence of the Good News.

David's first impulse, in contrast, was to trust God in every situation of his life. Even when he had every right to kill Saul in self-defence, David held back, preferring to let God do things his way (24:12). Have you been unfairly treated, betrayed or wronged by someone close to you? It rarely helps to lash out and give them a taste of their own medicine. Far better to pray, 'Lord, this is not fair and I'm angry about it, but I'm determined to make choices that please you'. You'll be amazed at how God can use that kind of honest trust in him to change even the most difficult situation (24:16–21).

APPLY   Think of some situations when you've been tempted. What was your first impulse? Think of one situation in which you need to be courageous and trust God. What will that require of you?

PRAY   Lord God, I want my first impulse to be a willingness to obey you. I can't do that in my own strength alone, so I ask that you fill me with your Spirit now and always.

35

Date: _____

Go for it, David!

PRAY 'I seek you with all my heart; do not let me stray from your commands. I have hidden your word in my heart that I might not sin against you' (Psalm 119:10,11).

READ 2 Samuel 5–7

REFLECT

We've now reached the high point in Israel's history. David is firmly established as king. He has soundly defeated his enemies (5:6-25), brought the Ark to Jerusalem (chapter 6) and led the chosen people into a time of peace (7:1) unprecedented in the history of Israel before or since. What would our world be like if there were more leaders like David today? Let's examine the plus points he built into his life during his struggle to the top.

David sought God's direction Notice the phrase, 'David enquired of the Lord' (5:19,23). Sometimes Christian leaders have difficulty doing that. When they become prominent, they start to believe their own press reports! But, as we've seen with Abraham, Moses, Joshua, Deborah and others, God is looking for men and women who seek and follow his direction.

David celebrated God's work Worship was an active and passionate activity for David (6:14,21). That's because he was so keenly aware of what God had done in his life. If you find your times of worship becoming dry or routine, the solution may not be to find a different church. You may need to get in touch with what God is doing around you. Then you'll have reason to shout!

David focused on God's priorities David's prayer (7:18–29) revealed a lot about his 'inner self'. He was genuinely humble, he knew that God was responsible for his success and, most of all, he showed his understanding of God's 'big picture' (7:23).

For all these reasons, David was Israel's greatest king. But his most significant legacy was something else; he became a forerunner of an even greater king who would be born many years later in a little town called Bethlehem.

APPLY Has God ever shaped your character through difficulties? How? Are you still applying those lessons today?

PRAY King Jesus, I worship and praise you with my whole heart right now. I want to follow your will for my life, wherever it takes me.

THE RISE OF ISRAEL: REVIEW

From the five readings in this section, summarise any significant insights and any thoughts on applying them to your life.

1

_____

_____

_____

2

_____

_____

_____

3

_____

_____

_____

4

_____

_____

_____

5

_____

_____

_____

Before you begin each new section you may find it helpful to read through your previous Review pages as a reminder of what God has been teaching you.

THE FALL OF ISRAEL

What goes up, must come down. At least that's the way it is for most things. Sadly, that was true for Israel. They had reached glorious heights under the reign of King David. And it looked as if the people God had chosen to be his own had finally made it. They had land, a king, peace and – best of all – a special relationship with the one true God.

But, as we shall see in our next five readings, the Israelites couldn't resist the temptation to disobey God's Law and to pursue the worship of idols. As a result, God allowed the Babylonians, Israel's ruthless and powerful neighbours, to inflict severe punishment on them.

But before we get too smug, we must admit that we have the same problem. As the saying goes, 'I can resist anything but temptation'. It's one of the great lessons of this section, that we all need God's help, and the help of fellow Christians, to avoid giving in to sin. And, as we'll see, even spiritual leaders need support and honest accountability to avoid the enemy's traps.

We see this revealed in the lives of three great Bible characters. King David committed adultery and arranged a murder at the pinnacle of his success. God forgave him and continued to use him as his chosen leader, but David lived with the consequences of his actions – strife and division in the family – for the rest of his life.

King Solomon, the wisest man who ever lived, couldn't resist the temptation to worship idols, if only a little. The problem was, he started a pattern of idolatry that got worse and worse with future kings. In the end, God had to put a stop to it, even though it had seemed like such a little thing at first.

And finally, we'll meet Elijah, one of the most courageous prophets in the Bible. He, too, has his flaws. After a successful showdown with the prophets of Baal, he goes AWOL and quits his job for God.

Sin may involve a public fall or a barely noticeable baby step. It may even cause us to run away from God. We must always be on our guard. The minute we think, 'Well, I'll never do *that*', is the time when we are most vulnerable to fall.

36

Sin in the spotlight

Date: _____

The fall of Israel

PRAY   You alone, O God, are worthy of praise and honour and glory. I worship you as I come to your Word today.

READ   2 Samuel 11:1–12:25

REFLECT

They say that when a Christian leader falls, it's usually caused by one of two things: money or morals. David didn't seem to have a problem with the former (1 Chronicles 29:1–20). Unfortunately he seemed to have a weakness with the latter, at least in this well-known instance. It's sad but true that a lifetime of positive achievement can be overshadowed by a temporary lapse in judgement.

How could David have done such a thing? How could 'the man after God's own heart', the man who showed so much courage in defeating Goliath, the man who exhibited such integrity in resisting Saul's paranoid attempts to kill him … how could that same person be so quick to commit adultery, arrange a murder and then abuse his position of power to cover it up?

The answer is the same for David as it is for us today. No matter how strong we may be, all of us have places in our lives that are weak to the pull of sin. That's why the biggest mistake we can make is to forget about sin, or to think it won't get to us. Often, the time we are most likely to stumble is just after we've made great spiritual progress. That's why it's so important to be part of a Christian community, one that knows us well enough to hold us accountable. Without that, even the strongest Christian can fall.

Another question that emerges from this passage is: why was David forgiven and Saul rejected? After all, both sinned against the Lord. The answer comes down to a single word: repentance. When David was confronted with his sin (12:1–10) he immediately and genuinely repented (12:13; Psalm 51). Sadly, Saul's response was to rationalise his actions (1 Samuel 13:1–15). It can be incredibly difficult and painful to admit our sin to others and to God. But when we do, God removes the burden and gives us a joy and closeness to him that we can experience in no other way.

APPLY   How do you react when you become aware of sin in your life? Has anyone ever been a 'Nathan' for you?

PRAY   'Search me, O God, and know my heart; test me and know my anxious thoughts. See if there is any offensive way in me, and lead me in the way everlasting' (Psalm 139: 23,24).

37

Wise guy

The fall of Israel

PRAY   Father, I eagerly look to your Word for guidance today. As I do, help me to be aware of your presence.

READ   1 Kings 2, 3

REFLECT

David really knew how to put pressure on his son. He publicly praised Solomon's wisdom, then charged him to settle some old scores for dear old dad (2:6). As it turned out, both of these themes played prominently in Solomon's life, as we shall see. There's no denying that a father's vision and encouragement (or lack of it) can have an enormous impact on the lives of his children. Whether you're a father or not, what kind of influence have you been in your family? What kind of influence would you like to be?

Solomon is best remembered for his uncommon wisdom (3:16–28). It's significant that although he showed impressive discipline in choosing it over other possibilities (3:9), Solomon's wisdom was still a gift from God (3:12). He instinctively knew that acknowledging God was the key to genuine understanding (Proverbs 1:7).

But Solomon made another choice in this passage that would ultimately lead to the fall of Israel. That choice is summed up in the word 'except' (3:3). For all his godly wisdom, Solomon opened the door to the worship of idols, something God clearly hated (Exodus 20:3–6). Often sin doesn't seem so bad at first. But a series of little steps can take us over the cliff as surely as one big leap.

We can take encouragement from the fact that even some of the Bible's greatest heroes – David and Solomon – had their weaknesses and made sinful choices. But the more encouraging thing is that even so, God was working out his plan (2:4) through them. David knew that the secret of staying in tune with that plan was to walk faithfully before God with all his heart and soul (2:4). That's still our challenge and opportunity every day.

APPLY   How would you *honestly* answer if God said to you, 'Ask for whatever you want me to give you' (3:5)? Why?

PRAY   Lord God, I've chosen to pursue so many things in my life. Give me a desire to know and follow you as my strongest ambition.

38

Date: _____

The heart of worship

PRAY   Lord, I often feel empty and unable to connect with you.
Please fill me with your Spirit so that I can worship you
today.

READ   1 Kings 8:1–9:9

REFLECT

Imagine how the people of Israel felt as they gathered for the dedication
of the new temple (8:1,2). For one thing, this was a spectacular building
(1 Kings 6; 7:13–51) and, for another, the king was going all out to celebrate (8:5,62,63). But as Solomon and his officials finished the ribbon
cutting ceremony, something strange happened (8:10). What made this
building so special?

Some may have thought it was the ark, which held the stone tablets con-
taining the Ten Commandments (8:6–9). They were a tangible reminder
of God's work in Israel's past. But the most important thing about this
building was that God showed up; he allowed his glory to fill the temple
(8:11). It's a powerful example of what true worship is all about.

It's natural to think of worship today in terms of the different features of
the service – the worship area, music, preaching, prayers and communion.
But what makes worship come alive is not just how well the service goes;
it's how prepared and eager we are to meet the living God. Even a 'bad'
church service can become good worship if we come with the right heart.
When you go to church, are you expecting God to be there?

Many years later, the apostle Peter used the image of the temple to describe
the Church, that is, all those who have decided to follow Jesus Christ
(1 Peter 2:5). Impressive as it was, Solomon's Temple was only temporary.
It was a preview of a much greater temple, the Body of Christ, that will last
forever.

At the end of Solomon's dedication ceremony, God warned the people to
remain faithful (9:1–9). He knew how quick they'd be to focus on the
mechanics of religion and forget about him. But the heart of worship is
not so much what we do – but who we meet.

APPLY   How would you describe your times of worship recently?
What makes your worship come alive?

PRAY   Lord Jesus, teach me to worship you from my inmost
being. You are great and holy and loving. Thank you for
giving me the opportunity to be part of your new temple.

39

Date: _____

PRAY   Lord, there are many voices competing for my attention right now. But the one voice I want to hear most is yours.

READ   1 Kings 16:29–19:18

REFLECT

If Solomon opened the door just a crack to idolatry (1 Kings 3:3), Ahab kicked it right in! He and his infamous wife, Jezebel, were leading the people of Israel down an evil path (16:29–33). That's why you have to cheer when Elijah challenged the prophets of Baal to a public showdown (18:22–24).

But the sacrifice on Mount Carmel was no pay-per-view event. Elijah rightly saw it as a struggle for the heart and soul of God's people (18:36,37). Throughout history, the Church has periodically drifted away from God and his priorities. There are many Christians today who feel like their denomination or church are on such a path. It takes wisdom and courage to challenge the Church, and we must be careful not to let our egos be the driving force. Of course, the best way to make a difference is through the integrity of our own witness.

One fascinating thing about this passage is that it introduces us to 'two Elijahs'. The first one is the bold, fearless prophet who won a dramatic victory for God. The other is a depressed, scared quitter who ran from God (19:1–9). The truth is, serving God is hard work. God sometimes allows us to have great successes, but because we are human we sometimes crash and burn. That's why, no matter how strong we are, it's important to take time for rest and renewal (19:7–9).

Ultimately, the thing that will sustain us most through the challenges of the Christian life is consistent, day-to-day communion with God. That comes from spending time reading his Word, praying and worshipping with other Christians. Those are the things that can re-ignite our hearts for the things of God. We should appreciate and remember the 'spiritual fireworks' when they happen. But the thing we need most is the ability to hear God's 'gentle whisper' (19:12).

APPLY   Have you experienced 'spiritual fireworks' in your Christian life recently? Have you heard God's 'gentle whisper'?

PRAY   Father, open my eyes to the ways I could be an influence for you in my world. I'm willing to trust you to make a difference through me.

40   A severe mercy?

Date: _____

The fall of Israel

PRAY   Lord, I'm really eager to hear what you have to say to me right now.

READ   2 Kings 25

REFLECT

This is not one of the Bible's most inspirational passages. In fact, it's a pretty depressing picture. Yet it's important because it marks the lowest point in the history of Israel so far. God's people had to learn the hard way that unchecked sin eventually brings devastating consequences. That's still true today.

As a result of Israel's wilful pursuit of idols, God allowed the Babylonians to be his instrument of judgement. And they exacted a heavy price: killing the leaders, smashing the glorious temple, burning Jerusalem and taking most of the people into captivity (25:21b).

Have you ever experienced a time of overwhelming disaster? Perhaps you've been shocked by the untimely death of someone you loved, a sudden financial reversal or unexpected news that you've been diagnosed with a serious illness. How do you react when your world falls apart?

Sometimes the only way forward is to look back to what God has done in the past. 'Lord, I'm miserable, I can't take it anymore and I see no way out. But you've been good to me in the past so I'm trusting that you won't abandon me now.' Take a minute to read Psalm 74, which is a prayer written by Asaph, one of those taken into captivity. You'll see that's exactly what he prayed.

If there's anything good about disaster, it's that we are forced to cling more tightly to God, simply because we have no other options. Writer Sheldon Vanauken referred to God's 'severe mercy' (*A Severe Mercy* Hodder 1977, 0340 24080 6) – the fact that sometimes God allows us to experience pain for a loving purpose that we could never see ahead of time (Revelation 3:19). God may shake you, but he won't abandon you. In fact, the very time you feel at your lowest may be the time when you are closest to God (Psalm 34:18).

APPLY   What have you learned from the disasters in your life? Has God drawn you closer to him through them? In what way?

PRAY   Father, I'm so thankful that you invite me to cast all my cares on you (1 Peter 5:7).

THE FALL OF ISRAEL: REVIEW

From the five readings in this section, summarise any significant insights and any thoughts on applying them to your life.

1

_____

_____

_____

2

_____

_____

_____

3

_____

_____

_____

4

_____

_____

_____

5

_____

_____

_____

Before you begin each new section you may find it helpful to read through your previous Review pages as a reminder of what God has been teaching you.

PSALMS AND PROVERBS

The Bible contains many kinds of writing and up until now we've been reading only history – the action-packed accounts of God's people journeying to become a great nation. Our next five readings, however, introduce us to two new kinds of biblical writing – poetry and wisdom literature.

The Psalms are essentially poetry written to express deep truths about God and his world. The person who wrote most of the Psalms – and many say the best – was King David. Our previous readings have shown us something of David's successes and failures. But in these three Psalms, we get a glimpse of how he felt. And, as you'll see, David had an incredible ability for expressing his feelings, both to us and to God. The passages remind us of King David's unique blend of talents; he was a shepherd, warrior, administrator, politician, spiritual leader and poet all in one!

The Book of Proverbs, on the other hand, is a collection of wise sayings primarily written by King Solomon. This fascinating Bible book breaks down into two basic sections: Chapters 1–9 are an extended father-to-son teaching on godly wisdom, while Chapters 10–31 are a collection of pithy statements each expressing a spiritual truth in a memorable way.

The truth is it's impossible to capture the wonder and richness of the Books of Psalms and Proverbs in five short readings. It would be well worth your time to read straight through the entirety of these wonderful books.

Over the years, I've often used a simple pattern for enjoying Psalms and Proverbs throughout the year. In addition to my regular Bible reading plan, if I have extra time I'll read five Psalms and one chapter of Proverbs each day. That enables me to read both books in a month. Or whenever I wake up in the middle of the night unable to sleep, I go downstairs and read the five Psalms and one chapter of Proverbs for that day. Often that's enough to redirect my mind and heart to a more peaceful place that allows me to go back to sleep.

Get ready to discover why Psalms and Proverbs have become two of the Bible's most popular books.

41

Date: _____

PRAY   Father, I want to focus on you today. I place at your feet all my cares and worries so that I can hear your voice.

READ   Psalm 23

REFLECT

I once participated in a group Bible study with people from around the world. We were studying Psalm 23, and the leader asked each of us to 're-translate' the opening verse in a way that made sense in our own culture. The responses were very revealing. From Latin America: 'The Lord is my friend, he helps me find work for the day'. From Russia: 'The Lord is my taxi-driver, he gets me safely through the streets of Moscow'. From Australia: 'The Lord is my loving mother, she takes care of me all day long'. From India: 'The Lord is my guru, he teaches me what I need to know'. How would you describe the Lord?

David compares him to a shepherd – a job he had personally experienced (1 Samuel 17:34). A shepherd both comforts (23:2,3) and protects (23:4) the sheep. No matter what happens, the shepherd stays with the sheep and actively works for their best interest. Have you experienced those things in your relationship with the Lord? Jesus picked up on this image in the New Testament, calling himself the 'Good Shepherd' (John 10:11–18).

But there is a second image in this much loved Psalm, one that seems a bit odd at first. David envisions himself at a banquet table, surrounded by his enemies (23:5)! He seems to be saying that even if the worst happens (23:4) we can trust that God will take care of us (Romans 8:28).

Another time, I was part of a group study on Psalm 23 in a prison. One of the inmates told us about his out-of-control life and about the crimes he had committed. In desperation, he had called his mother one day from prison asking for help. She told him, 'I don't know what to tell you, son, except read Psalm 23'. So he did, over and over again. As a result, he accepted Jesus Christ as his Saviour and Lord.

APPLY   Take a moment to 're-translate' the beginning of this psalm using images from your world. When are you most aware of God's presence?

PRAY   Lord, you know there are situations in life that cause me to be fearful. But I ask that you help me to sense your presence and trust your care so that I can face them in your strength.

42

David owns up

Psalms and Proverbs

PRAY   Lord, help me to be completely honest as I listen and speak with you today.

READ   Psalm 51

REFLECT

I once saw a television programme where commentators were discussing the impact of a prominent politician's confession of wrongdoing. 'He didn't go far enough on the "grovel-meter",' one said. 'If you're going to grovel, it doesn't work unless you go all the way.'

David's confession in this famous psalm certainly goes all the way. The context, as we have seen in a previous reading, is his sin with Bathsheba and against her husband Uriah (2 Samuel 11:1–12:25). Psalm 51 gives us an intimate look into the thoughts and feelings of 'the man after God's own heart' after he was confronted with his sin (2 Samuel 12:7,13). By carefully examining David's prayer, we can find three steps to genuine confession.

'Have mercy on me... ' (51:1) David didn't rationalise his actions. He honestly described them as 'transgressions ... iniquity ... sin'. Ouch! But that's true confession: completely admitting how we've disobeyed God. It makes no sense to hold anything back – God already knows what we've done.

'Cleanse me... ' (51:7) David realised that God sees sin as filthy. That's why he used the image of washing to describe forgiveness. We can't remove the stain of sin on our own. Only God can do that.

'Create in me a pure heart... ' (51:10) David's heart had been warped by his disobedience. So he asked God to straighten out his inner motives so he'd avoid future sin. After we've sinned, we need time for God to rebuild us from the inside out.

David knew that the worst thing about sin is that it separates us from God (51:11). But he also discovered the joy of putting on the clean clothes of forgiveness and experiencing close fellowship with God once again.

APPLY   Think of a time when you've been overwhelmed by a sense of your own sin. How did you relate to God during that time?

PRAY   'Create in me a clean heart, O God. Renew a right spirit within me. Do not banish me from your presence, and don't take your Holy Spirit from me. Restore to me again the joy of your salvation, and make me willing to obey you' (Psalm 51:10,11).

43

Praise the Lord!

Date: _____

PRAY   Lord, I praise you for who you are and for all that you've done in my life.

READ   Psalm 103

REFLECT

This is my favourite psalm. Why? Because it touches on so many of the great topics from the Old Testament in 22 concentrated verses: justice, Israel's history, God's compassion, forgiveness, human frailty and more. For me, reading this psalm brings to mind several of the Bible's greatest passages. Perhaps that's what David intended to do when he wrote it.

What makes David's poetry so powerful is that in it he speaks from the heart about his relationship with God. So let's see if we can discover some things in this psalm that will deepen our relationship with God today.

The benefits of God We don't usually think of it this way, but David reminds us that there are some incredible benefits to knowing God (103:2–5). The primary one is forgiveness of our sins. In the New Testament we'll see how God made this possible through the death of Jesus Christ on the cross. But living our lives God's way has positive effects in many areas. In fact, researchers today are discovering that people who pray are healthier. David didn't need an expensive study to figure that one out!

The character of God What is God like? The main traits David emphasises here are compassion (103:8,13) and a willingness to forgive (103:9–12). That's certainly reassuring. But, as Jesus reminded us in his model prayer (Luke 11:1–4), if we want to receive God's forgiveness ourselves, we must be willing to extend it to those around us. That's what 'godly character' is all about.

The response to God This psalm begins and ends with praise. When you really think about who God is, and all he's done for you, what else can you do? I particularly love the phrase 'all my inmost being' (103:1). I think of it sometimes when I'm in church. 'Father, from the depths of my heart and with everything I've got, I praise you today.' My challenge is to live each day as that kind of response to God.

APPLY   Do you have a favourite psalm? Can you list from your own experience the benefits of knowing God?

PRAY   Thank you, Father, for your compassion and forgiveness. Help me show those qualities to the people around me today.

44

Like father, like son

Date: _____

PRAY   Lord, I come to you as a child: I'm weak and I don't have all the answers. But I trust that you'll take care of me and give me what I need for today.

READ   Proverbs 1–4

REFLECT

When I was a child, the basement of our house had a bathroom that no one ever used. One day I noticed someone had pushed a desk and a chair into the small space between the sink and the shower. On the mirror was a card with a Bible verse printed on it, 'Speak Lord, for thy servant heareth' (1 Samuel 3:10). I realised that 'forgotten' room was the place my father went in the morning, before anyone was out of bed, to read his Bible and pray. That's how he taught me the importance of God's Word.

The Book of Proverbs contains the writings of Israel's King Solomon. As we've seen, God gave him a unique gift of wisdom (1 Kings 2,3). But underneath all the wise sayings is a father trying to teach his son how to live a godly life (1:8,10,15; 2:1–5; 3:1, etc). That's the most important job any father will ever have.

Solomon's main point is that wisdom is the foundation for godly living, whether we are a son or a daughter. It's a wisdom that begins with 'the fear of the Lord' (1:7; 2:5). Not fear in the sense of panic or dread. Rather, our relationship with God should be characterised by reverence, obedience and trust. Is that how you relate to God?

Godly wisdom also produces several benefits. It *protects* us against evil and its consequences (1:10–19) and it *provides* us with happiness and health (3:13–26). That's why it's worth pursing. But it's important to note that Solomon is talking about wisdom that's more than just head knowledge. True wisdom is a heart commitment to learn and follow God's ways (4:23).

A wonderful detail in this passage is Solomon's reference to the godly influence of his father and mother – David and Bathsheba (4:3,4). All parents make mistakes, but it's never too late to begin teaching our children godly wisdom by our words and example.

APPLY   How would you characterise your relationship with your earthly father? With your heavenly Father? How have you learned about God's wisdom?

PRAY   Father, I want to live a life that pleases you. Help me to demonstrate your wisdom in my words and my actions.

45

A treasure chest of wisdom

Date: _____

Psalms and Proverbs

PRAY   Lord, there are so many things I need to learn about you.
Help me do that as I read and pray today.

READ   Proverbs 16–18

REFLECT

When I was growing up, my parents tried several strategies for having
'family devotions'. One of the things that worked best was reading
Proverbs after dinner. We went around the table, each person reading one
verse aloud until we finished a chapter. Then my mother would ask, 'So,
which verse struck you today and why?' Before we could go outside to play
we had to give a *thoughtful* answer. I confess, the most 'meaningful' verse
for me was usually the last one I read!

Which of these verses was most meaningful to you today? The wonderful
thing about the Book of Proverbs is that it's like a treasure chest full of little
jewels. It's amazing to me today that I still remember many of the proverbs
we read around the dinner table. God's Word has a way of sinking in
(Psalm 119:11). What seem like individual verses actually fit together into
at least three big themes:

Wisdom and folly When he wrote Proverbs 16:16, Solomon may have been
thinking of the choice he made years earlier (1 Kings 3:4–15). Of all the
wise things we can do, using our words for positive ends is one of the most
significant.

Humility and pride Solomon's most famous statement on this theme is
Proverbs 16:18. A humble, contented life is far more satisfying than grab-
bing all we can get. We all learn this lesson sooner or later.

God's will and human action God expects us to use our talents and abilities,
but the paradox is that the final results depend on him (16:1–4). Getting
that truth out of balance can tempt us into either inaction or pride. God
wants us to act in dependence on him.

APPLY   What wisdom have you gained from your experiences in
life and your relationship with God? Try making up one or
two proverbs of your own.

PRAY   'O Lord my God ... I am only a little child and do not
know how to carry out my duties .... So give your servant a
discerning heart ... to distinguish between right and
wrong' (1 Kings 3:7–9).

PSALMS AND PROVERBS: REVIEW

From the five readings in this section, summarise any significant insights and any thoughts on applying them to your life.

1

_____

_____

_____

2

_____

_____

_____

3

_____

_____

_____

4

_____

_____

_____

5

_____

_____

_____

Before you begin each new section you may find it helpful to read through your previous Review pages as a reminder of what God has been teaching you.

THE PROPHETS

What do you think of when someone says, 'He's a prophet for our times'? A long-haired radical with a sign saying *THE END IS NEAR*? An insightful commentator about social issues? A lone figure courageously standing up to injustice through civil disobedience?

In a sense, the Prophets of the Bible were all of those things. They warned of judgement to come, wrote critiques of their society and, as a result, were forced to stand in opposition to the powers of their day. But there is one other significant thing about biblical prophets that distinguishes them: they spoke for God (2 Peter 1:20,21). That's what gave them their greatest power.

Up until this point, we've been reading mostly history, with some poetry and wisdom literature in our last section. But our next five readings introduce us to a new genre of biblical writing: prophecy. The Old Testament includes 16 prophetic books and there are different ways to categorise them. The most popular is according to length: the Major Prophets (Isaiah, Jeremiah, Ezekiel and Daniel) and the Minor Prophets (the last 12 books of the Old Testament with all the odd names!).

Another way to divide them is by their relationship to a significant historical event: Israel's defeat and exile into Babylon. If a prophet was 'pre-exilic' (such as Hosea, Joel or Amos) they tended to focus on denouncing sin and warning of the coming Day of the Lord. If they were 'post-exilic' (such as Haggai or Zechariah) they tended to focus on hope and restoration for the broken people of God. Some long-lived prophets were active before and after the exile and their writings cover both of these themes (such as Isaiah).

Another fascinating aspect of the prophetic books is the life stories of the prophets themselves. What was it like to be a prophet? We'll read the dramatic personal stories of three of them: Jeremiah, Daniel and Jonah. As you'll see, being a prophet is a tough, thankless job.

There's one last feature of the prophetic books that you'll want to keep an eye on: they often point to a coming of a Messiah, a Saviour that would appear many years later. You'll find many such references, but the most concentrated is Isaiah 52:13–53:12, which we'll cover in our readings.

The prophetic books are passionate, hard-hitting and very relevant to our world today. Get ready to be challenged!

46

The suffering servant

Date: _____

PRAY   Lord, make me receptive to the specific message you have for me today.

READ   Isaiah 51–53

REFLECT

When it comes to Old Testament Prophets, Isaiah is the heavyweight. Not only is his book of prophecy the longest, but also it's one of the most quoted in the New Testament. Isaiah's ministry outlasted several kings (Isaiah 1:1), both before and after the exile, and his writings covered at length two great themes of Old Testament prophecy – warning and judgement (chapters 1–39), and hope and salvation (chapters 40–66).

This reading comes from the hopeful half of Isaiah, and refers to a time when God's people were in desperate need of hope. As we've discovered, Israel's idolatry and sin brought a terrible punishment (2 Kings 25). And, worst of all, they were afraid God had finally given up on them (Psalm 74:1,9). But God inspired Isaiah with a message of hope that is as relevant today as it was thirteen centuries ago.

God will save his people (Isaiah 51:1–52:12) As the people languished in Babylonian exile, Isaiah pointed to the big picture, to what God had done for them in the past (51:1,2). That's a good place to start when you feel you've strayed from God. Next, Isaiah emphasised God's willingness and power to save. That may be hard to believe when you've really messed up. But the truth is God loves it when sinners return to him (Luke 15:11–32). That's Good News for God's people then and now (52:7).

God will send a Saviour (Isaiah 52:13–53:12) The incredible thing about this section (aside from the fact that it was written 800 years before Christ!) is the description of the kind of saviour God would send. Not a forceful, military conqueror. Rather, a suffering servant, wounded and broken for our sins (53:5). The only way for us to be saved, to get rid of our sin problem, was for someone else to take the punishment for us. And that's exactly what Jesus did on the cross.

APPLY   Are there areas of your life where you are losing hope? How does this passage help? How would you describe God's 'big picture' for you?

PRAY   Lord Jesus, thank you for dying for me. Your love is so amazing! I praise you with my whole heart.

47

Date: _____

PRAY   God, you are truly great – and yet you care about me and want to be in touch with me. Thank you.

READ   Jeremiah 1:1–3:5

REFLECT

Jeremiah had a tough assignment. He was young and knew he was a pathetic speaker (1:6). Yet God chose him to confront the leaders of his day with a frightening message. No wonder he tried to chicken out. But that's what makes this book so interesting; it combines a powerful message with a candid personal story.

Jeremiah was a young priest, apparently content to fulfill his duties in a small, country 'parish' (1:1). But God had bigger plans for him, calling him to be 'a prophet to the nations' (1:5). It's natural to think God will use the most talented or successful people to do his work. But that assumes God is dependent on our abilities. In fact, he has the power to do far more than we could ever imagine. All he needs is people who are faithful and willing to follow when he calls.

Notice God's personal interest in Jeremiah (1:5). You may think God doesn't really know or care about you. But that's not true. The Creator of the universe was thinking about you before you were even born. With a single verse (1:5), God sweeps away the modern debate about when life begins and gives every life – including yours – a God-given purpose.

That doesn't mean life will always be easy. Jeremiah had the difficult task of telling his own people that God was about to unleash a terrible punishment (1:14–16) in response to their idolatry (1:16; 2:11–19). And what a graphic image he uses to describe it – a bride who becomes a prostitute (2:1–3:5). The worst thing about sin is not just that we've broken God's rules. It's that we've broken our relationship with him.

But that's not the end of the story. God's love is so great that he's willing to forgive and 're-marry' his wayward people (Jeremiah 31:31–34). As we'll soon discover in our New Testament readings, sending Jesus Christ to earth was God's plan for winning back the hearts of his people (Galatians 4:4–7).

APPLY   What things in life draw you away from God? When do you feel most passionate about your relationship with God?

PRAY   Lord Jesus, forgive me for the times when I fail to value you most of all. I offer you my worship, praise and love.

48   Dare to be a Daniel

Date: _____   *The prophets*

PRAY   'Praise be to the Lord, to God our Saviour, who daily bears our burdens' (Psalm 68:19).

READ   Daniel 6

REFLECT

Our readings in Isaiah and Jeremiah gave us the bleak context for this passage in Daniel. Israel's idolatry had produced national defeat and exile for God's people. No doubt many in Daniel's generation would have been tempted to give up, to assume they had no chance in life. But Daniel wasn't worried by his negative circumstances. He made it his number one priority to develop a deeper relationship with God and then trusted that God would use him however he saw fit (chapter 1).

As a result, Daniel found himself in a prominent government position (6:1–3). It is interesting that Daniel was perfectly willing to work for a secular king. It's a mistake to think that full time Christian service is the only way to make a difference for God. Certainly God calls some to be pastors and Christian workers. But he calls others to be in the marketplace or government. In fact, people who are willing to live out their faith with courage in secular situations can have a spiritual impact that no full time Christian worker could ever have (6:25–27).

But standing up for God brings opposition, in Daniel's case from jealous beaurocrats (6:4–9). When we face similar attacks in the workplace it may seem like 'business as usual'. But often there's an element of spiritual opposition involved. Daniel seems to understand this, since his first reaction is to get away and pray (6:10). Is that your response to opposition, too? You may never have to face a den of lions for your faith – but you will face other difficulties. Daniel was willing to sacrifice his entire career because he trusted God no matter what (6:23). That was the key to his 'success' and yours.

APPLY   What would it mean for you to trust God no matter what in your day-to-day work? How could you follow Daniel's example in taking more time for private prayer during your day?

PRAY   Lord, I want to be a bolder witness for you. Please give me the strength and courage to stand up for you through my words and actions each day.

49

Date: _____

PRAY   Lord, I'm stepping out of my hectic life into your calm presence. Fill my mind and heart with the things you know I need to hear.

READ   Jonah 1–4

REFLECT

There are many reasons why people take cruises, but Jonah's has to be the most unique. 'Guess what? I'm running away from God' (1:10). So begins this delightful book that reads more like a four-act play than prophetic literature.

Act One: Running from God We're too sophisticated today to believe we can run away from God. Right? But Jonah's trip to Tarshish is no more ridiculous than when *we* sin and act as if it's a secret. Sin is like that. It causes us to do things we know are not right (1:12, Romans 7:7–25) and then convinces us 'there's nothing wrong with it' (4:2).

Act Two: Prayer for salvation Jonah was swallowed by a great fish (1:17–2:1) and although it gets a big laugh in the Sunday School play, it must have been a terrifying experience (2:3–6). Coming face to face with the consequences of our sin can be overwhelming. At such times, our sin-warped rationalisations are stripped away and we realise our only hope is to cry, 'Lord save me!' Jonah's experience also symbolises our need for salvation.

Act Three: Revival in Nineveh What's encouraging about this chapter is that God gives everyone a second chance. Failing doesn't disqualify us from God's service. Being unwilling to repent does that. The Ninevites turned from their wicked ways and believed God. It was the same act of faith that God honoured in Abraham (Jonah 3:5; Genesis 15:6).

Act Four: Disappointment with God This 'play' might have stood more chance of being a West End hit if it had ended after the third act! But that's not real life; sometimes things happen that cause us to question God. However, Jonah's temper tantrum gives God yet another chance to demonstrate his patience and love. Some people believe the God of the Old Testament is harsh and unforgiving ... in spite of the evidence to the contrary. Even Jonah knew that (4:2).

APPLY   Have you ever been disappointed with God? Why? What restored your trust in him?

PRAY   'But with shouts of praise, I will offer a sacrifice to you, my Lord. I will keep my promise, because you are the one with power to save' (Jonah 2:9).

50   **Great is your faithfulness**

Date: _____   *The prophets*

PRAY   'I remember the days of long ago; I meditate on all your works and consider what your hands have done' (Psalm 143:5). Thank you, Lord God, for the many things you've taught me about yourself in the Old Testament.

READ   Malachi 1–4

REFLECT

The Book of Malachi is a tough read. It's a blunt exposé of Israel's culture of unfaithfulness in the years following the exile. After all God had done for his people, Israel can't seem to resist the temptation to go their own way. (For a quick review of Israel's history, read Psalms 105 and 106.)

We find several examples of this theme in our reading today, but three have particular relevance. First, the Israelites had become insincere in their worship (1:7–14). That's what happens when we try to reduce our relationship with God to a religious routine. Merely going through the motions is offensive to God (1:10) because it shows we're out of touch with the true heart of worship (Deuteronomy 6:4,5).

Secondly, Malachi singles out men for not remaining committed to their wives (2:10–16). The prophet reminds them of the need to guard both their actions and their spirits (2:15, Matthew 5:27–30), a challenge that is especially poignant today with the opportunities for sin present on the Internet. Finally, Malachi hammers his people for their unfaithfulness in the area of tithing – 'robbing' is what God calls it (3:6–18). Strong words. But let's consider that only a handful of Christians today give the biblically-prescribed minimum of ten percent of their income to the local church, and many give next to nothing – just their loose change! Malachi ends with two full volume passages on 'the Day of the Lord' (2:17–3:5; 4:1–6). Chosen people or not, sin eventually brings judgement.

As we come to the end of the Old Testament, we have to conclude that there's got to be a better way for people to relate to God. No matter how hard we try, we can't fix the sin problem on our own. But hang in there. The Good News is coming soon.

APPLY   What things weaken your resolve to remain faithful to God? What helps you love God with all your mind, soul and strength?

PRAY   Lord, you've been so faithful to me. I want to show my gratitude through the sincerity of my worship and the integrity of my actions.

THE PROPHETS: REVIEW

From the five readings in this section, summarise any significant insights
and any thoughts on applying them to your life.

1

_____

_____

_____

2

_____

_____

_____

3

_____

_____

_____

4

_____

_____

_____

5

_____

_____

_____

Before you begin each new section you may find it helpful to read through
your previous Review pages as a reminder of what God has been teaching
you.

CONGRATULATIONS!

You have completed the first part of the E100 Challenge.

In the Old Testament we have seen how God longed to have a close relationship with people from the very moment he created them. Repeated failure on their part resulted in a succession of loving acts initiated by God, designed to draw people back to himself – the greatest of which we'll discover as we now move into the New Testament.

The following 50 readings will complete the big picture of God's plan right through to its ultimate fulfilment as Christ returns and a new heaven and new earth are established.

So, don't stop now! There's so much more! Get ready for the next part of the journey as **Essential 100** leads us into the life of Jesus.

THE LIVING WORD

So, you've made it halfway through the **Essential 100**! After 50 readings through the Old Testament you are ready to launch into the New Testament. And of course the key focus of your next 50 readings is one person – Jesus Christ.

Ever since Adam and Eve disobeyed God in the Garden of Eden, God has been working out his plan of salvation. So far, most of that plan has involved the people of Israel, the Jewish nation. We've seen how God revealed himself to them through signs and wonders in Egypt, through giving them the Law and then through the message of the Prophets. But, as we finished the Old Testament, we had the sense that something was still missing. God's people kept turning away from him. They just couldn't get right with God on their own.

That's why he took the dramatic step of sending his own Son, Jesus Christ, to earth. What God had been saying to his people for years and years in a variety of ways, he now said in person (Hebrews 1:1–3). It would be hard to understate the significance of that single event. In fact, the coming of Jesus Christ is the most important moment in all of human history.

But that also introduces the most important question in all of human history, one that every person will eventually have to answer: 'Who is Jesus?' (Luke 9:18–27). As you'll see immediately you begin your next five readings, the New Testament is very clear on the answer. Jesus is God in the flesh (John 1:14), the promised Messiah who came to earth to save us from our sins (John 1:29–34).

Of course, many people are unwilling to accept what the Bible teaches about Jesus. Perhaps C S Lewis offered the best response to such a view in his classic book, *Mere Christianity*. He writes:

I am trying here to prevent anyone from saying the really foolish thing that people often say about Him: 'I'm ready to accept Jesus as a great moral teacher, but I don't accept his claim to be God'. That is the one thing we must not say. A man who was merely a man and said the sort of things Jesus said would not be a great moral teacher. He would either be a lunatic – on a level with a man who says he is a poached egg – or else he would be the Devil of Hell. You must make your choice. Either this man was and is the Son of God: or else a madman or something worse. You can shut him up for a fool, you can spit at Him and kill Him as a demon; or you can fall at his feet and call Him Lord and God. But let us not come with any patronising nonsense about His being a great human teacher. He has not left that open to us. He did not intend to. (Mere Christianity, MacMillan Publishing Company, 1943).

51

In the beginning – again

Date: _____

PRAY   Father, I would like to encounter your Son, Jesus Christ, in a new and real way today.

READ   John 1:1–18

REFLECT

'OK … there was this man named Jesus and I'm writing this to tell you about all the really great things he did.' That's how I would have started my gospel account. But not John; he started way above the clouds (1:1–5) – before time, before creation, before anything.

His opening phrase, 'In the beginning… ' (1:1) parallels the first verse of Genesis. John wanted us to know that the coming of Jesus was as significant as the creation of the world; it was literally the start of a new creation (2 Corinthians 5:17). He used a somewhat mysterious phrase, 'the Word' (1:1), to describe Jesus. The point is, what God had been saying to humankind from a distance for so many years – through creation, through signs and wonders, through the Law and the Prophets – he now says in person. Jesus Christ was God himself (1:1,14), the living Word. If you want to know what God is like, look at Jesus.

The sad thing was that people still didn't get it! They didn't understand who Jesus really was (1:5,10). That's still true today. Many accept him as a good man or a great moral teacher or even a unique model of team building and leadership. But unless you also accept him as God (1:14), it's the same thing as rejecting him (1:11).

The Good News is that God loves us and through Jesus has made a way for all people to become his children (1:12). No longer is our relationship with God dependent on sacrifices or keeping a detailed set of laws, as we saw in the Old Testament (1:17a). All God wants us to do is 'receive' and 'believe' Jesus. That's how we can discover the incredible blessings God wants to give us (1:16,17) – the best being a personal relationship with him for all eternity. Is that what you want?

APPLY   Can you honestly say that you have received and believed Jesus?

PRAY   Father, it's mind-boggling to think that you came to this earth because you wanted a relationship with me. I do receive and believe in Jesus. Please draw me closer to you today.

52

Date: _____

PRAY 'My soul glorifies the Lord and my spirit rejoices in God my Saviour, for he has been mindful of the humble state of his servant . . .' (Luke 1:46–48).

READ Luke 1

REFLECT

It must have been an exciting family gathering when Elizabeth and Mary met (1:39,40). Not only were both women pregnant as a result of miraculous circumstances, but both realised God had chosen them for something special. God often uses unlikely people to do his work. You may feel too old, like Elizabeth (1:18), or too insignificant, like Mary (1:48). But God can do incredible things (1:37) through people who are faithful and humbly dependent on him (1:6,13,50). No matter where you are in life, God can use you if you've developed those qualities.

But when God chooses us, we must be ready to respond. Compare Zechariah's 'How *can* I be sure of this?' (1:18), with Mary's 'How *will* this be?' (1:34). Mary believed God could do it; Zechariah wasn't so sure. Having faith doesn't mean you will understand exactly what God is doing in your life. Very often, you won't. Faith is simply believing that God has the power to do anything (1:37) and then committing yourself to his way, no matter what happens (1:38).

Sometimes the life of faith can lead us down a lonely road. We can become discouraged, wondering if anyone notices our attempts to follow God. But Gabriel pulled back the curtains of heaven and gave us a wonderful glimpse of God personally listening to our prayers (1:13) and taking note of our attempts to live for him (1:28–30). Living the Christian life can be a challenge but the encouraging thing is that you are never alone.

Gabriel's primary job was to announce that God was ready to make the big move in his plan of salvation (1:30–35). We've been following that plan since Adam and Eve first sinned in the Garden of Eden. The exciting thing about the New Testament is that God steps into history and makes the plan happen himself. That's the 'big story'.

APPLY Do you ever feel isolated or discouraged in your attempts to follow God? When and why? What things make you feel that God cares after all?

PRAY Father God, it's true that I sometimes don't understand what you are doing in my life. But I believe you have the power to do incredible things through me and I'm ready if you want to use me today.

53

Show-stopping truth

Date: _____

PRAY   'Hark! the herald angels sing, glory to the newborn king.'
Lord, no matter what day of the year it is, I'm so thankful
for what you did for me at that first Christmas.

READ   Luke 2:1–40

REFLECT

Whenever I read this passage, I can't help thinking about the classic
Charlie Brown Christmas Special on television, where Linus walks onto an
empty stage and recites from the second chapter of Luke. He ends by
saying simply, 'That's what Christmas is all about, Charlie Brown'. The
show-stopping truth is that God came to earth.

It's incredible to think that the Saviour of the world would make his
entrance in this way: an inconvenient, messy birth in a stable (2:6,7).
That's no way to get good ratings, or to get noticed at all. But God intentionally chose to work his greatest miracle through 'invisible people' like
some overwhelmed parents and terrified shepherds.

It's a mistake to assume that God prefers media stars and prominent people
to accomplish his purposes. That's a danger for those of us who live in the
western world. Even in our local churches, we sometimes act as if the
clergy are the only ones through whom God can work. Certainly God has
given pastors and other Christian leaders a special and important calling
(1 Timothy 3). But the healthiest churches are those that encourage everyone, regardless of their position or natural abilities, to use their spiritual
gifts for the benefit of all (1 Corinthians 12).

Look what happened to the shepherds. Possibly they stumbled from the
fields to the stable, smelling of sheep and totally bewildered at being
dropped into the role of ambassadors for God. What did they know about
prophecy or God's plan of salvation? All they knew was that their lives had
been changed by an incredible time of worship (2:13,14) and an opportunity to meet Jesus (2:15,16). That experience transformed them into effective evangelists who had a powerful impact for God (2:17). And that's what
the Church is all about, Charlie Brown!

APPLY   Would you say that Jesus has transformed your life? Why
and how?

PRAY   Lord Jesus, I worship and praise you today. Please give me
the courage and ability to share with others what you've
done in my life.

54   The world's greatest prophet

Date: _____

PRAY   Lord, please prepare my heart and mind to receive your
word to me with joy today.

READ   Luke 3

REFLECT

John the Baptist was the quintessential biblical prophet. He lived in the
desert (3:2), ate natural food and wore rough clothes (Matthew 3:4). But
the most important thing about him was that 'the word of the Lord came
to him' (3:2). As we discovered in our Old Testament readings, God called
prophets to the difficult task of announcing his message of both judgement and hope.

But John the Baptist had an extra assignment: he was to prepare the way
for the Messiah (3:4). As it turned out, the 'Anointed One' was his cousin,
Jesus. John the Baptist deserves credit for recognising God's work in a
member of his family. It's sometimes difficult to encourage the spiritual
growth in our siblings or extended family because we 'know each other too
well'. But your family members are the ones you'll be the closest to in life
and the ones on whom you can have the biggest spiritual influence.

John had a big influence on Jesus. Notice the main elements of his message
– a call to repentance and a challenge to produce fruit, all in preparation
for the coming of the Christ (3:7–14). Later in his own ministry, Jesus
preached his famous 'six woes' sermon (Luke 11:37–54), which had the
same tone, and many of the same words and themes as John the Baptist's
message here. Jesus even went so far as to say that John the Baptist was the
greatest prophet (Luke 7:24–28).

In the end, John devoted his life to the higher purpose of humbly point-
ing people to Jesus (3:15–17; John 3:27–36). You may not be a gutsy
prophet or a fiery preacher, but you can still have a big impact for God by
letting your words and actions point others toward Jesus.

APPLY   In what ways could you influence your family members for
God's priorities? Would any of your family patterns have to
change in order to do that? How has your family
influenced your faith?

PRAY   Lord God, sometimes I feel like 'a voice calling in the
desert'. But with your help, I'll stand up for you in my
family, work and community.

55   **Lead us not into temptation**

Date: _____

PRAY   I'm so grateful for your love, Father God. Feed me from your Word today so that I may live a life that pleases you.

READ   Matthew 3:13–4:17

REFLECT

Why did Jesus need to be baptised by John? They both knew he didn't need it. After all, Jesus was the Son of God and without sin. So John's baptism of repentance was unnecessary. The key is found in the word 'fulfil' (3:15). Jesus' mission was to take the sin of the world – including yours and mine – on himself (John 1:29). His life on earth was devoted to fulfilling that mission and, as a result, he received the affirmation of his heavenly Father (3:17).

What a shock it must have been for Jesus to go directly from the close fellowship with God to the traps Satan had prepared in the desert (4:1). But after a time of spiritual growth (or even *during* a time of spiritual growth) is often when the enemy chooses to pounce. Your temptations may not be as dramatic as the ones Jesus faced. Yours may simply be expressing angry words with your spouse or colleagues in a weak moment, pursuing an unhealthy relationship when you are tired and needy, or even becoming proud about your spiritual progress. But if you're growing in your relationship with God, watch out! Satan will try to disrupt you and convince you that you're a spiritual phoney. Perhaps that's why even Jesus got away for a time of prayer after periods of intense spiritual activity (Mark 1:32–35).

It's helpful to notice what Jesus did to avoid Satan's temptations. Each time, Jesus went back to the Word of God, the Bible. It gave him the solid ground he needed to make the right choices (4:4). The same is true for us today. Notice that the Bible can protect us, as it did Jesus. But it can also mislead us if we misuse it, as Satan attempted to do (4:5,6). That's why it's important to be part of a Christ-centred, Bible-believing church. It's much easier to stay on track when you are accountable to a faithful community of fellow Christians. Don't try to walk through the desert by yourself.

APPLY   When do you feel closest to God? When are you most susceptible to temptation? What steps could you take to prepare for the temptations that will come your way this week?

PRAY   Lord, forgive me for the many times I've given in to temptation. With the help of your Word and your Spirit, I want to please you with my words, thoughts and actions today.

THE LIVING WORD: REVIEW

From the five readings in this section, summarise any significant insights and any thoughts on applying them to your life.

1

_____

_____

_____

2

_____

_____

_____

3

_____

_____

_____

4

_____

_____

_____

5

_____

_____

_____

Before you begin each new section you may find it helpful to read through your previous Review pages as a reminder of what God has been teaching you.

THE TEACHINGS OF JESUS

Imagine you were alive when Jesus was on earth. And imagine you had the opportunity to hear him teach. Perhaps you were on the hillside when he preached the Sermon on the Mount; or you were in the crowd when he told one of his insightful parables. Now imagine that you have come home for the night and as you enter the house, someone in your family says, 'So, what did he have to say?' How would you summarise the teachings of Jesus?

That's the impossible challenge we now face – to capture the essence of Jesus' teaching in five short readings. And Jesus was always teaching, because he knew that his actions spoke as loud, if not louder, than his words.

For example, one of our readings in this section includes 'The Lord's Prayer' (Matthew 6:9–13). But Jesus' most powerful teaching on prayer may not have been this model prayer. Instead, it was his lifestyle of prayer. Notice what triggered the disciples' interest in prayer (Luke 11:1a). As we read the Gospels we find frequent references to Jesus' pattern of prayer (Mark 1:35).

Jesus practised what he preached and that's one thing that gave him credibility as a teacher (Matthew 5:19b). Of course, the main factor was that he was God in the flesh. His listeners didn't understand that yet. But the more he taught, the more they realised he was unique (Matthew 7:28,29).

Our readings focus on the preaching and parables of Jesus. The Sermon on the Mount is unquestionably the greatest sermon ever preached. Jesus delivered it early in his ministry just as he was starting to come to public attention. Instead of giving the crowds 'feel good' soundbites, he gave them a full dose of moral and ethical teaching that called people to the highest standard possible (Matthew 5:48). Jesus never 'dumbed down' his message.

As for the parables, Jesus knew that telling stories about common things and familiar situations of life would help him connect with his listeners. It also enabled him to point out the hypocrisy and sin of the religious leaders who opposed him, without seeming overly confrontational.

Preaching and storytelling combined with a consistent lifestyle – that was Jesus' masterful formula for getting his point across, as you'll see.

56

Radical happiness

Date: _____

PRAY 'May the words of my mouth and the meditation of my heart be pleasing in your sight, O Lord, my Rock and my Redeemer' (Psalm 19:14).

READ Matthew 5:1–6:4

REFLECT

When people think about the Sermon on the Mount today, they often refer to it as 'The Beatitudes' because of the nine 'blessed' statements Jesus made at the opening of this passage (5:1–12). The word 'beatitude' means 'blessed', or literally 'happy'. In other words, Jesus begins the world's greatest sermon by defining true happiness. Sounds like a winner.

The problem is, all he talked about was losers – the poor in spirit, people in mourning, the meek and persecuted. No one wants to be around people like that. But, according to Jesus, the way to be happy is to go out of our way to include those who are troubled. Jesus loved the down and out and, if we want to be his followers, so should we.

He then tackled another touchy subject: influencing others (5:13–16). Today, many people believe that the most important thing about religion is to keep it private. For them, privacy is more essential than truth. But Jesus challenged his followers to be like *salt* – flavouring and preserving the world with the gospel – and *light* – demonstrating the gospel with godly actions. Once you've discovered 'the way, the truth and the life' (John 14:6), there's no way to keep it hidden (5:14,15). As Francis of Assisi once said, 'Preach the gospel all the time. Use words when necessary'.

Jesus continued by taking on some even tougher topics – murder, adultery, divorce, revenge and more (5:21–48). In each case he referred to the teachings of the Law ('You have heard that it was said… ') and then raised the stakes by zeroing in on the source of the problem: the heart (5:28). Following a list of rules does no good without a heart that's committed to the right motivation – reconciliation, faithfulness, forgiveness and love. These are the things Jesus valued most.

APPLY What makes you happy? Which part of the Sermon on the Mount is the most challenging to you? Why?

PRAY Lord, pursuing happiness takes up a lot of my time and energy. Perhaps too much? Help me to have right priorities.

57 The audience of One

Date: _____

PRAY   Lord God, I praise and worship you that you know everything I need for this day and are committed to loving me.

READ   Matthew 6:5–7:29

REFLECT

You can tell Jesus never went to Bible college. If he had, he would have begun his sermon with a joke, worked through three points and ended with a punchy quote. But Jesus was on a mission; he had three short years to communicate everything his heavenly Father wanted him to say to the world. And after that, he faced the cross. So he packed everything in.

One of his most important teachings was about prayer. The Lord's Prayer (6:9–15) is undoubtedly the world's most famous prayer; it combines two perspectives that can help us today. First, in prayer we look beyond ourselves to God: his nature, his holiness, his kingdom and his will. Second, we focus on day-to-day issues: food, forgiveness, and strength to avoid temptation. At the very least, prayer involves worshipping and requesting. Without a balance of these two perspectives, our prayers become lopsided and eventually less effective.

But for Jesus, prayer wasn't just a verbal formula. It was the natural extension of a lifestyle focused on doing his Father's will. Notice how many times Jesus refers to 'your Father' in the second half of this sermon (6:6,8,18,32, etc). Whether he's talking about prayer or fasting or giving or any other subject, the point is we are to do all things with our Father God in mind. Or as writer Os Guinness has put it, we are to play to 'the audience of One'. When that becomes the central focus of our lives, worries about things like money, possessions, clothes or food all take their proper place (6:33).

Jesus concluded his Sermon on the Mount with more straight talk: forgive or else (6:14,15), don't judge others (7:1–6), watch out for false prophets (7:15–20). And he saved his toughest word for the end (7:21–23). There's a big difference between feeling good and being 'blessed' (5:1–12).

APPLY   What do you suppose Jesus would have to say to people walking through your local shopping centre today?

PRAY   Conclude your quiet time by slowly saying the Lord's Prayer, stopping to reflect on each phrase.

58   **D-Day for sin**

Date: _____

PRAY   Lord, there are so many things that prevent your Word from taking root in my life. Help me to set them aside so that I may receive your Word today.

READ   Matthew 13

REFLECT

On the stormy morning of June 6, 1944, England and her allies began a massive effort to liberate Europe from the grip of Nazi Germany. At great cost of human life, the Allied Forces invaded the beaches of Normandy, France, and over the next year gradually reclaimed the captured territory and defeated the enemy regime.

D-Day provides a perfect picture of the kingdom of heaven. Ever since Adam and Eve disobeyed God in the Garden of Eden, the world has been under the influence of sin. But when Jesus 'invaded' the earth, it was the beginning of the end for Satan's evil empire. Theologians describe the kingdom of heaven as 'the rule of God's grace in the world'. As Jesus went about his public ministry, he liberated more and more people from sin and expanded his kingdom on earth. And through his death on the cross, he opened the way for everyone to enter his kingdom.

But that was a hard concept for people to see at the time, which is why Jesus used so many common analogies. By comparing the kingdom of heaven to things like yeast, hidden treasure, a mustard seed or a net, Jesus painted a picture of a seemingly insignificant thing that would have an overwhelming impact. That's how it is when we decide to follow Jesus – it seems like a small step at first, but over time it changes everything about our lives, both now and for eternity.

We must be careful, however, not to allow our consideration of the kingdom of heaven to become a mere intellectual exercise. Jesus challenged his hearers to 'understand with their hearts' (13:15). That means we allow his Word to sink in and affect our attitudes, motivations and actions. Inhabitants of God's kingdom are committed to being both hearers and doers of his Word (James 1:22–25).

APPLY   How has it changed your life to be in God's kingdom? Or have you yet to take that first step?

PRAY   Father, thank you for inviting me into your kingdom. I want to allow your Word to sink deeper and deeper into my heart so that I can bear fruit for you.

59

Date: _____

The uncommon deed

PRAY   Holy Spirit, I invite you to be present with me as I explore this passage.

READ   Luke 10:25–37

REFLECT

This passage has special significance to me since my home church is called Church of the Good Samaritan. In the entrance lobby of the building we have a life-size, contemporary statue of one person helping another up, poignantly symbolising this parable and our church's motto, 'Doing the uncommon deed in the name of Jesus Christ'.

On the surface, the man in Jesus' story asked a thoughtful question about the next life (10:25). But he wasn't completely satisfied with Jesus' answer, so he pressed for a guarantee (10:29). At times, we too feel the tendency to reduce God's generous love to a mere formula. But it doesn't work that way. If your relationship with God is too heavily defined by a list of dos and don'ts, you'll have trouble being passionate in your love for God or joyful in your service to others. Jesus doesn't seem too interested in the man's 'perceived need' either. Zeroing in on the real need, he tells the well-known parable, from which I'd like to make two points.

First, the outcast was the hero. No one liked or respected Samaritans, but Jesus says that this despised outcast does a better job of understanding and expressing God's love than anyone else, including the religious experts. Christian faith is not about being an expert or being perfect all the time. It's about being willing to receive God's love and forgiveness and being able to express it to those around us.

Secondly – and this is also the punch line of the story – the true neighbour is the person who shows mercy. The word 'mercy' carries with it both the idea of a feeling of empathy and compassion, as well as taking action on behalf of those who are helpless. A Christian who has all the right answers but who does not show mercy is not an effective witness for God (Luke 6:36).

APPLY   Who needs mercy from you? How could you express it to them today?

PRAY   Lord God, thank you for showing incredible mercy to me. With your help, I intend to do the same for others today.

60

Date: _____

Lost property

The teachings of Jesus

PRAY Lord Jesus, I want to draw closer to you today. Please give me a deeper understanding of why you died on the cross for me.

READ Luke 15

REFLECT

I once saw a cartoon that showed two clergymen scowling at a third who was striding purposefully into his crowded church. The one frowning cleric said to the other, 'Yes, but it's the *way* he saves souls that makes my blood boil!'

It's easy for Christian leaders to feel the kind of professional jealousy and theological snobbery that we see in our passage today (15:1,2). But we can get off track too, when we view the Church as a club for those who have got it all together – or who think they have. Jesus' image of the Church was more like a 'lost property cupboard'. That's the point of the stories about the lost sheep and lost coin (15:3–10). The whole reason Jesus came was to reclaim lost and broken people. The Pharisees just didn't get it!

In his third story (15:11–32), Jesus gives us a glimpse into God's heart – he loves sinners and is waiting for them to return to him. You'd think the father would have given his prodigal son a sound beating, or at least scolded him, before welcoming him back. But, contrary to what we think, God is far more interested in repentance than punishment. In fact, Jesus defined true repentance when he passionately quoted the younger brother (15:17–19). Is that how you feel when you recognise your own sin?

You have to feel sorry for the resentful older brother. He felt the father's love should be reserved only for the few who earned it – especially him. But if that's how God felt, no one would be saved. The mission of the Church of Jesus Christ is not to isolate the 'good' people, it's to welcome and save the 'bad' people. And which of us really fits into that first category?

APPLY Think of a time when you truly repented from the heart. How did that experience make you feel about God? Who feels welcome in your church? Do you ever make the mistake of trying to earn God's love?

PRAY Father, forgive me when I'm like the older brother. You've been so generous with your love for me. Help me to share some of that love with the struggling people around me.

THE TEACHINGS OF JESUS: REVIEW

From the five readings in this section, summarise any significant insights and any thoughts on applying them to your life.

1

_____
_____
_____

2

_____
_____
_____

3

_____
_____
_____

4

_____
_____
_____

5

_____
_____
_____

Before you begin each new section you may find it helpful to read through your previous Review pages as a reminder of what God has been teaching you.

THE MIRACLES OF JESUS

I used to love the films of Woody Allen. He's famous for making comedies that portray hapless bumblers (with himself playing the lead) struggling with the questions of life, death and God. In one film, Allen sarcastically says, 'If I could only see a real miracle, then I could believe'. But I've discovered that Woody Allen's characters never believe – they just keep searching. These days I have trouble watching Woody Allen films because I wonder if he even wants to find the answer. For me, there's no humour in a dead end.

But, as we'll discover in our next five readings, simply seeing is not always believing. Jesus performed all kinds of miracles. He healed lame and blind people, walked on water and changed the weather, exorcised demons and brought dead people back to life. This caused many to put their faith and trust in him. But seeing the miraculous caused others, like the religious leaders, to oppose him. The fact is, if we've already decided not to believe, no amount of proof will change our minds.

Author and speaker Josh McDowell is a person who wrestled hard with the questions of life, death and God. He went on a search for answers, and tried to be honest about his assumptions. McDowell set out to prove that Jesus was not divine and that Christianity was bogus. He researched and studied everything he could. He lined up enormous amounts of data. But in the end, he concluded that his original assumption was wrong. The evidence pointed to one conclusion: Jesus Christ was who he claimed to be – the Son of God, Saviour and Lord of all.

In his book *Evidence that Demands a Verdict*, (Authentic Lifestyle 1 89893 863 6) McDowell notes that a well-known philosopher compared faith to a 'leap in the dark'. But after honestly evaluating the data, Josh McDowell said that for him, coming to faith in Jesus Christ was like 'a leap into the light'.

Jesus linked his teaching with miracles (Matthew 4:23) and instructed his disciples to do the same (Luke 9:1,2). It was a powerful combination. But the biggest miracle of all was when he himself came back to life after dying for our sins on the cross. That's the big miracle that validated everything he said and did.

61

All you can eat

Date: _____

The miracles of Jesus

PRAY 'Blessed Lord, who hast caused all holy Scriptures to be written for our learning: Grant that we may in such wise hear them, read, mark, learn, and inwardly digest them... ' (The Book of Common Prayer).

READ Luke 9:1–36

REFLECT

Any politician or youth leader can tell you the secret of attracting a large crowd: free food! But Jesus was no politician and his miraculous feeding of 5,000 men (not to mention the thousands of women and children who were undoubtedly present) had tremendous significance both for the disciples and for us.

To fully understand this miracle, we must consider its context. As we have already discovered, Jesus had been preaching about the kingdom of heaven (Matthew 13). He now sends the disciples out with the same message (9:1,2). 'You've seen how I do it – now you give it a try.' Some people today are offended by the idea of evangelism. But Jesus didn't ask his followers to impose a set of personal beliefs on others. He simply asked them to heal people and share the Good News (9:6).

When the disciples returned, Jesus took them aside for fellowship and debriefing (9:10), a good model for those involved in ministry. And that's when he chose to feed the large crowd. It would be nice to know how it happened. Did a stack of loaves drop out of the sky? Did the bread miraculously replenish itself as people pulled off pieces? The text only says, 'They all ate and were satisfied... ' (9:17). But the point is, Jesus had given his followers an unforgettable symbol of what he had been teaching them: that God's kingdom multiplies as it is given away.

This miracle also demonstrated another important truth: Jesus really was the Son of God. Peter understood sooner than anyone else (9:20). And about a week later, God confirmed it for Peter, John and James in the quintessential 'mountaintop experience' (9:28–36). Jesus didn't miraculously create food to attract a crowd. He did it to drive home an important message. 'I am God in the flesh. I am here to establish a kingdom that must grow. I need you to tell others all about it.'

APPLY How do you feel about sharing God's Good News with others?

PRAY Father, you've given me so much through your Son, Jesus Christ. With your help, I'm ready to share that Good News with others.

62   Imaginative faith

Date: _____

The miracles of Jesus

PRAY   Lord Jesus, my mind and heart are full of the pressures and problems of life. Help me to set them aside so that I can be with you.

READ   Matthew 14:22–36

REFLECT

Several years ago, I was involved in a situation that caused me great stress. The problem was so big that I thought I'd never get out of it. At my lowest point, I read this passage and taped a copy of Jesus' words to the wall beside my desk. After that, whenever I felt fearful, I'd say this verse out loud: 'Take courage! It is I. Don't be afraid' (14:27). It took several years, but God miraculously resolved my problem.

Some people act as if becoming a Christian exempts them from life's problems. Unfortunately, that's not true. But, no matter how bad things get, God never abandons us. If we are willing to reach out to him, the moment of crisis can become the time of closest fellowship with God.

A lot has been made of Peter's lack of faith on the lake (14:30,31), but I'm impressed with his imagination under such pressure. Sometimes faith requires imagination – the willingness to believe God can do things that seem impossible (Matthew 19:26). Unlike Peter, I would never have imagined that I could walk on water; I would have stayed in the boat.

God won't give us everything we wish for. But we can trust God to provide everything we need, when we need it, if we stay focused on him.

With all the drama of the storm, it would be easy to overlook what Jesus was doing before he walked on the water; he was spending 'quality time' with his Father (14:23). What do you like to do when you have time to yourself? It would have been easy for Jesus to let his early successes go to his head (14:13–21), or to be overwhelmed by the pressures of ministry (14:22–36). That's why he needed to spend time alone in prayer. And if Jesus needed prayer to stay spiritually focused and renewed, we need it even more.

APPLY   What are your biggest problems? What makes you fearful? What could you do to seek God in the midst of your storm?

PRAY   Lord, you know there are some problems in my life that I'd love you to solve. But, even more than that, I want to experience you with me. That's my prayer today.

63

I see what you mean!

Date: _____

The miracles of Jesus

PRAY   Father, 'Open my eyes that I may see wonderful things in your law' (Psalm 119:18).

READ   John 9

REFLECT

Sometimes people who are the most religious are also the most resistant to a genuine work of God. That's what we see in this passage. After hearing about the miraculous healing of a blind man (9:6,7), the religious leaders responded with scepticism. The problem was that they were more interested in their rules than the reality of what God had done (9:16).

What causes good people to resist God's work? Sometimes it's fear of the unknown or a legitimate desire to avoid being misled. But we should be careful if we feel a resistance to spiritual things just because they do not fit our way of thinking. Sometimes the most honest thing we can say is, 'This is outside my experience, but I'm open to whatever God wants to show me' (Acts 5:38,39). That kind of honesty can open the door to a deeper understanding of God.

The disciples tried to analyse the blind man's predicament (9:1,2). Sometimes sin *can* be the cause of sickness. But Jesus reminds us that often he has reasons for allowing things that aren't always apparent to us (9:3–5), and that's good news for those experiencing illness or disease today. How might that affect the way you pray for people you love?

In the midst of all the arguing, the blind man had the clearest insight of all. Note the progression of his faith. He started with a basic understanding of the facts (9:11,25), formed an opinion about Jesus (9:17) and finally made a decision to believe (9:38), in spite of the consequences (9:34). That's a good description of how to become a Christian. Jesus welcomes the tough questions of honest seekers (9:35–37). But he is not so patient with those who use their doubts as a way of avoiding the truth (9:39–41).

APPLY   How would you trace the progression of faith in your life? Do you have any honest questions about Jesus? Who could help you sort them out?

PRAY   Lord Jesus, thank you for opening my eyes to the truth about you. Help me to share that truth with others, through my words and actions.

64   **In the name of Jesus**

Date: _____

The miracles of Jesus

PRAY   Lord, you are powerful and mighty and above all things. And yet, you know and love me. Thank you!

READ   Mark 5:1–20

REFLECT

Whenever I drive past a pornography shop or psychic centre, I feel aware of the reality of evil. At these times, I often sing a song my mother taught me when I was a child, 'In the name of Jesus, by the power of God/ The enemy flees, the enemy flees'. It's my way of claiming God's protection and announcing his authority over evil.

The demon-possessed man in our passage knew the reality of evil (5:1–5), and it was destroying his life. That's Satan's agenda – to capture and destroy God's creation. Some people think the devil is comical. But evil is no joke and we are all vulnerable to attack (1 Peter 5:8). Yet, for all his destructive powers, Satan knows who the higher power really is. When Jesus came to earth, Satan was defeated and he knows it (5:6,7).

You'd think the people would have cheered when Jesus healed the demon-possessed man. No more howling at night, no more danger to the community. But they weren't happy; they were afraid (5:15). Why? Perhaps they were more comfortable with the status quo. 'Oh, that's just how he is.' But Jesus wants to bring the most radical kind of healing into our lives; he wants to break our addiction to sin. And that can be unsettling.

Jesus also wants to empower us to share the Good News. Notice that he didn't spend time teaching the man released from demon possession. He didn't need to. All he told him was, 'Go… tell them how much the Lord has done for you, and how he has had mercy on you'(5:19). A changed life is still the clearest and most powerful statement of the gospel there is.

APPLY   In what ways, if any, have you become addicted to sin? How could you open yourself to God's radical healing power in your life?

PRAY   Lord Jesus, I invite you into those places in my life where the enemy still has a grip. Please free me from the chains that hold me, so that I may serve you with my whole heart.

65

Dead man walking

Date: _____

PRAY   I don't like to think about death, Lord. But as I explore your Word today, give me a new appreciation of how you've overcome death and offered me new life.

READ   John 11

REFLECT

As far as the religious leaders were concerned, this miracle was the straw that broke the camel's back. When Jesus brought Lazarus back to life, the chief priests and Pharisees decided they had to kill Jesus (11:53). What made this miracle so threatening to the religious establishment?

The answer lay in the political situation. The leaders feared anything that would cause the Romans to take away the symbols of their national identity (11:48). Allowing ourselves to value anything more than the one, true God – even good things like church and country – can have disastrous implications. Our world is full of wars that are the result of this very mistake.

But Jesus didn't care too much about politics. He cared about people. One feature that stands out in this passage is the compassion of Jesus. He really loved people (11:3,5,36). And what an impact his love had on Martha. In an earlier encounter with Jesus, Martha came off as a fussy complainer (Luke 10:38–42). Now she's the first one to respond to him (11:20). Unlike the religious leaders, Martha put Jesus at the centre of her life and priorities.

There was a deeper reality to this miracle. Jesus knew that he was going to die and that God would bring him back to life. By raising Lazarus, he created an unforgettable symbol of the new life, eternal life, that he would offer to those who believed in him (11:25,26). The irony is that the religious leaders made this very point without realising it (11:50). How sad that people can 'be religious' all their lives and still not understand who Jesus is. Martha didn't understand everything either; but she honestly stated what she did understand (11:24) and then trusted herself and her future to Jesus (11:27). That's all he asks us to do.

APPLY   Is there anything about Jesus that threatens you? Is there anything you love more than Jesus?

PRAY   Yes, Lord, I believe you are the Christ, the Son of God. And I believe you are the resurrection and the life. Thank you for offering that new and eternal life to me.

THE MIRACLES OF JESUS: REVIEW

From the five readings in this section, summarise any significant insights and any thoughts on applying them to your life.

1

_____

_____

_____

2

_____

_____

_____

3

_____

_____

_____

4

_____

_____

_____

5

_____

_____

_____

Before you begin each new section you may find it helpful to read through your previous Review pages as a reminder of what God has been teaching you.

THE CROSS OF CHRIST

The cross is surely the most recognised and reproduced symbol in the history of the world. Not only is it used in Christian settings such as in churches and stained glass windows or on Bibles and prayer books, but it has also become popular in secular settings such as in jewellery or as a 'lucky charm' for the car mirror. What's so important about the cross?

Of course, the main reason is because Jesus Christ was executed on a cross. That single event was literally the crossroads of time and eternity. It was on the cross that Jesus died for the sins of the world, thereby making a way for all people to have a relationship with God, one that would last forever.

But the popularity of the cross has perhaps blurred the horror of how it was originally used. When Jesus was on earth, the Romans used crucifixion as a way of punishing criminals or humiliating enemies of the state. Either way, it was a gruesome form of public execution. Victims were usually whipped first and forced to carry the crossbeam to the place of execution. They were then nailed to the beam, which was hoisted up on a stake. Death was a slow, agonising process and usually came from loss of blood or suffocation. A modern symbol that captures some of the horror of the cross is the electric chair, although no one would consider wearing that as jewellery.

Jesus knew exactly what he was in for (Luke 9:18–22). And even though his mission on earth was to die on the cross, it was still a struggle (Mark 14:32–42). But he did it – first, because it was his Father's will and second, because it was the only way to pay the price for sin, once and for all. Without the cross there could be no salvation.

Jesus never intended the cross to become a fashion statement. For him, it was a symbol of all-out commitment from his followers. As he said, '. . . anyone who does not carry his cross and follow me cannot be my disciple' (Luke 14:27). And, as you'll see in the rest of the New Testament, the early Church clearly understood the significance of the cross (Philippians 2:5–11; Galatians 2:20; Romans 6:5–11).

Your next five readings take you to the very heart of God's plan of salvation – the 'big story' we've been following through the Bible.

66

A meal to remember

Date: _____

The cross of Christ

PRAY   Jesus, you are the bread of life (John 6:25–40). Please satisfy my hunger for God as I spend time with you today.

READ   Luke 22:1–46

REFLECT

In his famous painting entitled *The Sacrament of the Last Supper*, Salvador Dali portrayed the upper room as a spotless, surreal, almost other-worldly setting. But when we look carefully at this passage, we see that the reality was more down to earth: a borrowed room, a dinner cooked by men, lots of arguing around the table and one person with a dark secret.

Why did Jesus bother with this awkward party? Why not just excuse himself from the bickering for an early bedtime? The answer can be found in a single word: 'fulfilment' (22:16). Everything that the Law and sacrifices had symbolised, everything that the Prophets had predicted, everything that we've read in the Old Testament, pointed to what was about to happen. Jesus was there to fulfil the mission given to him by his Father – to die on the cross for the sins of the world.

That's the message he wanted to symbolise for his followers with this meal. The bread helps us remember his body (22:19), the fact that he was about to 'be broken' for sin. And the wine helps us remember his blood (22:20), the fact that he was about to make the final sacrifice for the forgiveness of sin. He called it a 'new covenant', that is, a new agreement between God and people that would last forever.

In all this, Jesus singled out two people for special attention. Even though Judas was planning a betrayal, Jesus gave him several opportunities to change his mind (22:21–23; Matthew 26:20–25), all of which he ignored. And when Peter spoke up with characteristic bravado (22:33), Jesus set in motion the biggest lesson of his life (22:34, 54–62; John 21:15–19). At this special meal, when Jesus had the weight of the world on his shoulders (22:39–46), he still cared for individual people – including you and me. That's the motivating compassion that took him to the cross.

APPLY   What do you think about when you take communion in your church? What things do you 'remember' about Jesus?

PRAY   Lord Jesus, I won't forget what you did for me through your body and blood. I'm so thankful that I can have a new and living relationship with you.

67

The big decision

Date: _____

The cross of Christ

PRAY   Father, open my mind and prepare my heart so that I can worship you 'in spirit and in truth'.

READ   John 18

REFLECT

Some people think Judas' motive in betraying Jesus was not hate or greed, but impatience. Perhaps Judas had grown tired of waiting for Jesus to make a move, so he tried to force him to fight (18:1–3). 'Use your power to set up a kingdom... now!' Whatever Judas' motive may have been, things spiralled out of control.

The trial that followed was hardly the enactment of proper legal process. The religious leaders broke every rule of fairness, because they had already made up their minds about the verdict (18:30,31). That's what happens when we let hate control us. If you have any unresolved anger in your life, you'd be wise to get to the bottom of it before it damages your relationship with others and with God.

Pilate certainly didn't care about fairness; he just wanted to avoid hassle (18:29–35). It doesn't seem like he cared too much about truth either (18:38). For many people today, a fuzzy notion of 'tolerance' has replaced the reality of truth. 'What's true for you may not be true for me.' Jesus cut through that kind of thinking with clarity. 'Everyone on the side of truth listens to me' (18:37). Unless we stay connected to the Word of God we'll wander further and further from the truth. That's why reading the Bible is so important.

Before he knew it, Pilate was faced with the most important decision of all time – what to do with Jesus? Sooner or later, everyone must make that decision for themselves. Is Jesus a source of anger and frustration; is he a hassle to be avoided; or is he 'the way, the truth and the life' (John 14:6)? Think carefully: it's the biggest decision you'll ever make.

APPLY   Do you believe there is such a thing as 'absolute truth'? How would you discuss this with those who believe differently?

PRAY   Lord Jesus, I want to be on the side of your truth. Help me to increase my ability to hear and my willingness to obey your voice.

68

Paid in full!

The cross of Christ

PRAY   O God, I begin this time with you by confessing my sins.
Thank you that you are willing and able to forgive and
cleanse me.

READ   John 19

REFLECT

John's account of the crucifixion reads like a top news story; it's full of
vivid detail. Yet he didn't sensationalise what happened. He just let the
facts speak for themselves. It's hard to fully comprehend the torture that
Jesus endured – flogging, thorns jammed into his scalp, punches in the
face, nails through his hands and feet, a spear wound from point blank
range. It was a gruesome murder. But in those days crucifixion was
common, so this one may not even have made the front page.

There's one angle to the story that comes through loud and clear: the religious leaders hated Jesus. Screaming for his execution, they were like
wolves circling for the kill (19:6–16). It's a wonder no one stopped to ask
them, 'If it's true, as you say, that he's not the Son of God, why are you so
worried about him?' It's a good question to ask anyone who vehemently
opposes Jesus today. Finally even Pilate realised what was driving the religious leaders and in his own weak way he said, 'Enough's enough!' (19:22).

But the significance of the cross goes far beyond the historical facts. Just
before he died, Jesus shouted, 'It is finished' (19:30). Some may have
thought it was the final word of a beaten man. But in the Greek the literal
meaning of the word Jesus used was, 'Paid in full' – the same word that was
stamped on a paid invoice. Instead of a dying gasp, Jesus' last word was a
triumphant shout. 'I've paid the price, the full price for all time for the sins
of the world. Death no longer has the final say. The kingdom of darkness
is defeated. I've completed my mission. It is finished!'

One interesting extra feature to John's news article is the story of
Nicodemus (19:39). He didn't seem to respond to Jesus during their first
encounter (John 3:1–21). But at the foot of the cross, the truth finally
made sense and this religious leader broke from his angry colleagues and
publicly identified himself as a follower of Jesus. At the foot of the cross –
that's where everything finally makes sense.

APPLY   Are you a secret disciple? Why? What is the significance of
the cross in your life?

PRAY   Lord Jesus, I thank you for all that you endured on the
cross for me. Today and every day I want to publicly
identify myself as your follower.

69   The linchpin

Date: _____   *The cross of Christ*

PRAY   Father, 'I want to know Christ and the power of his resurrection' (Philippians 3:10). Open my heart as I read your Word today.

READ   John 20,21

REFLECT

The resurrection of Jesus Christ is the linchpin of the Christian faith. If you eliminate that, as many have tried, everything falls apart. The apostle Paul acknowledged this when he said, 'And if Christ has not been raised, our preaching is useless and so is your faith' (1 Corinthians 15:14). So it's important to understand the significance of the resurrection, and that's what the people in our reading today are struggling to do.

Mary Magdalene was the first one to the tomb (20:1). Her love for Jesus was so deep that she was beyond the point of worrying who knew about it (20:10–17). Does that describe your love for Jesus? John had experienced the love of Jesus, too (John 13:23) and he had responded by being a faithful follower. But, deep down, he was still confused (20:9). Do you ever feel that way? Maybe you've been a churchgoer for years, but something is missing? John had his real conversion experience when he made a decision to believe in Jesus based on the evidence (20:8). Have you made that kind of decision about Jesus?

Thomas was walking the fine line between intellectual honesty and self-centred rejection. 'Unless *I* see ... *I* will not believe' (20:25). Sometimes our pride can prevent us from understanding more about God. Fortunately, Thomas didn't stay that way (20:28). Is there anything preventing you from becoming a fully committed follower of Jesus Christ? As for Peter, he didn't know if he was still a follower of Jesus or not (Luke 22:54–62). But, on the beach, Jesus restored him and gave him a new mission in life (21:15–19).

There's no getting around it: the resurrection of Jesus Christ is fundamental to Christian faith.

APPLY   For you, what is the most convincing evidence for the resurrection of Jesus Christ?

PRAY   My God, I marvel at the miracle of the empty tomb. Thank you for winning the battle over sin, death and hell... for me.

70

Goodbye ... for now

Date: _____

PRAY   Lord, I want to know the reality of you in my life. I'm really eager to meet with you today.

READ   Acts 1:1–11

REFLECT

Jesus went to great lengths to prove that he had risen from the dead (John 20:30,31; 21:25). He left a trail of evidence so that everyone, including you and me, would be able to understand what he had done on the cross and in the tomb. The odd thing is, the disciples *still* didn't get it; they were still looking for a political kingdom (1:6).

Sometimes it's hard to let go of our own ideas and let God begin to work. It can be confusing and even painful, but until we give up our own plans, we can't experience God's. Jesus didn't have much time left on earth so he didn't waste it correcting the disciples. He just took his last shot at communicating two important realities about his kingdom.

The first is *power*. There was no way the disciples would be able to fulfill the mission Jesus was about to give them (Matthew 28:18–20) on their own. They needed his presence and power – and that's why he promised the Holy Spirit. Some people today over-emphasise the Holy Spirit, almost making him more important than Jesus. Others seem to be afraid of the Holy Spirit and act as if he's not allowed to work anymore. The bottom line is that Jesus said we need the Holy Spirit's help and we should be eager to ask for it.

The second reality is *witnessing*. The reason for the power was to communicate a message (1:8). And note that Jesus told them to wait (1:4). Sometimes waiting for the Holy Spirit to create an opportunity for ministry is difficult. But real results come when we prayerfully wait to get a sense of what the Holy Spirit wants us to do.

We can only imagine what Jesus' ascension to heaven looked like. No doubt it left an unforgettable impression on the disciples and confirmed everything Jesus had taught them. And the wonderful thing is, someday we won't have to use our imagination. We'll be able to see Jesus for ourselves (1:11).

APPLY   What does it mean for a Christian to live 'with the end in mind'?

PRAY   Jesus, your name is above all others. I bow my knees and confess that you are my Lord forever (Philippians 2:9–11). I look forward to the day when I'll see you face to face.

THE CROSS OF CHRIST: REVIEW

From the five readings in this section, summarise any significant insights and any thoughts on applying them to your life.

1

2

3

4

5

Before you begin each new section you may find it helpful to read through your previous Review pages as a reminder of what God has been teaching you.

THE CHURCH IS BORN

No matter where you go in the world today, you can find some kind of church building to worship in. The question is, especially in Western countries, will you find any people in those churches? How did the Church get started and what is it supposed to do?

Our next five readings take us back to the very beginnings of the Church and help us understand its origins and purpose. Our last readings on *The cross of Christ* left the disciples reeling from the whirlwind of Jesus' death, resurrection and ascension. They had no idea what would happen next. All Jesus said before he returned to heaven was, 'Wait' (Acts 1:4). Wait? Wait for what?

As it turned out, Jesus was preparing to send them an incredible gift, the Holy Spirit, who was 'poured out' on all people on the day of Pentecost. That event empowered Jesus' followers and ignited an evangelism explosion. It was the birth of the Church.

So what is the Church? Some people think the Church is a particular denomination or a building. Some act as if the Church is a chain of social clubs for good people. The essence of the Church is far more profound. The Church is literally a union of Jesus and all those who have decided to follow him.

And the mission of the Church is to share the Good News of salvation with all people. This wasn't so clear at first. Because God had developed a special relationship with the Jewish people, many thought salvation was only for them. But God stepped in at Pentecost and blew the doors wide open. The gospel and the Church are open to everyone.

Once Jesus' followers got that straight, the Church began to grow by thousands of people each day. It was out-of-control growth and not even opposition or persecution could stop it. In fact, those things only accelerated its growth.

So why are so many churches nearly empty today? Perhaps it's because they've lost sight of the original mission of the Church. So your challenge as you dig into the next five readings is to rediscover what that mission is.

71

A surprise gift

Date: _____

The Church is born

PRAY   Jesus, thank you for promising to send your Holy Spirit.
           I'm waiting and open for whatever you want to show me.

READ   Acts 2

REFLECT

How would you feel if you were one of the disciples at this point? For three
years, you've been at the centre of the biggest story in the world. You heard
Jesus preach and saw his miracles. You watched his crucifixion and witnessed his resurrection and ascension. But how do you feel now that it's
all over? And what was going to happen next?

The disciples couldn't answer those questions, so they returned to a familiar routine (2:1), gathering to worship on the day of Pentecost (which was
a Jewish harvest feast). That's a good thing to do after a big crisis – get with
other believers and worship God. Sometimes the only way to make sense
of the things that happen in our lives is to wait in the presence of God.

In this case, the disciples' waiting led to an incredible spiritual break-
through – the unleashing of the Holy Spirit (2:2–4). Because the Holy
Spirit is part of the Trinity (Father, Son and Holy Spirit), he has been
present and active since the beginning of time (Genesis 1:2). But at
Pentecost, he was 'poured out' on all who believe in Jesus (2:38), not just
a select few. And when the Holy Spirit enters your life, you're never the
same again.

Peter is an example of how the Holy Spirit completely changes a person.
He had always been a 'ready, fire, aim!' kind of guy, and that had got him
into trouble more than once. But the Holy Spirit changed Peter from an
impulsive deserter to a persuasive leader in the newly born Church. And
note how the Holy Spirit did it. He gave Peter insight into God's Word, a
keen understanding of God's plan, uncommon courage and power, plus a
supernatural effectiveness in ministry (2:40,41). Those are the characteris-
tics of a person who's been filled with the Holy Spirit.

APPLY   How have you experienced the presence and work of the
           Holy Spirit in your life?

PRAY   Come, Holy Spirit, fill me with your insight and power so
           that I can become an effective witness to the reality of
           Jesus Christ.

72   A completely different team

Date: _____

PRAY   Father, I want to leave my past behind and get on with the business of being in your team. I'm ready for you to use me any way you want to.

READ   Acts 3:1 – 4:37

REFLECT

Have you ever watched a sporting event, say a football match, where the underdog team is getting punished in the first half – only to see them come back to win the game in the second half? That's what it's like for the disciples in our passage today. The 'defeat' of the cross is behind them and the Holy Spirit has moulded them into a completely different team that was destined to change the course of history.

It would have been natural for Peter to think, 'Jesus was the team captain all these years while I did the following. Now it's my turn to get the spotlight.' But Peter still remembered the 'half time pep talk' Jesus had given years earlier (Luke 9:1,2) and he wasted no time putting it into action. Empowered by the Holy Spirit, Peter healed a lame man and preached another powerful sermon. And he did so with a Jesus-focused humility (3:6,11–26) that even the religious leaders recognised (4:13). That's what happens when we let the Holy Spirit empower us to share the Good News.

But not everyone was happy about the disciples' dramatic comeback (4:1–7). The fact is, when God begins to work in his Church, there will be opposition. You can expect it in your life and in your church. But opposition can't stop the Church – in fact, opposition makes it grow (4:23–35), as many anti-Christian governments in recent times have discovered. What stops the Church dead in her tracks is when Christians don't focus on Jesus, don't witness for their faith, and don't rely on the power of the Holy Spirit.

Some think that the most unique thing about the early Church was their approach to money and possessions (4:32–37). It was certainly impressive and challenges our commitment to giving today. But it seems that their willingness to practice 'radical sharing' was the result of an even more impressive trait: unity (4:32). Imagine what the Church could do today if they were 'one in heart and mind'.

APPLY   How close is the Church today to being 'one in heart and mind'? What could you do to encourage unity in your own church?

PRAY   Lord, enable me 'to spread your word with great boldness …. and (to) perform miraculous signs and wonders through the name of your holy servant Jesus' (Acts 4:30).

73   Seeds in the wind

Date: _____   *The Church is born*

PRAY   Jesus, as I begin my time with you, I want to confess my sins and ask for your forgiveness. Also, bring to mind any people that I need to forgive.

READ   Acts 6:8–8:8

REFLECT

Stephen was a great leader in the early Church (6:5,8) but he broke all the rules for guest preachers. His sermon was well beyond twenty minutes, his text was way too long (he tried to explain the entire Bible) and he finished with some high-volume, personal accusations. You'll never get a return invitation with that kind of message.

But God had given Stephen that message for the religious leaders and, tragically, they weren't in the least bit interested. For one thing they were too angry. Sometimes people use anger to hide an inner struggle with God. If you find yourself getting angry a lot, it might be worth asking yourself, 'Is there something God is saying to me that I'm afraid to hear?'

The other reason they weren't open to Stephen's message was that they loved their religion more than they loved God (6:13,14). There's nothing wrong with appreciating your church and its traditions. But watch out if they become too important to you. It has been said many times and it's still true: Jesus never came to start a religion; he came to start a relationship. With you.

Stephen became the Church's first martyr. His stoning was a horrible expression of hatred (7:54–58). Yet God had a purpose for even this brutal act: to spread the message of salvation even further (8:4). The persecution unleashed that day was like a tornado to a dandelion; it spread the seeds everywhere (8:1–3). It also brought to the surface a young man who will feature prominently in the remainder of the New Testament (8:1,3). Although it would take some time and a dramatic encounter with Jesus, the angry Saul would become the apostle Paul, a man destined to become the greatest evangelist of the early Church. We should never doubt the power of God to change a life.

APPLY   Have you ever been persecuted for your faith? How did you react? Is an absence of persecution indicative of anything important?

PRAY   Lord, I want to stand up for you boldly even though I sometimes feel hesitant. Please give me the courage to seize the moment for you.

74

Date: _____

PRAY   Lord, thank you for the Bible. Please help me both to understand and apply what I learn from it today.

READ   Acts 8:26–40

REFLECT

Philip wasn't one of the big name stars of the early Church. Compared to top of the bill apostles like Peter or Paul, he had more of a walk-on part. Maybe that's how you feel at times. But the success of the Church is not dependent on celebrities. It's dependent on ordinary people who are empowered by the Holy Spirit to become extraordinary witnesses for Jesus Christ.

That's what we see in this passage. Philip was just minding his own business when an angel (8:26) and the Spirit (8:29) orchestrated an opportunity for him to share the Good News. We must never lose sight of the fact that God is already at work in the world. Our job is to be sensitive to what he's doing and willing to let him use us at the right time.

So what can we learn about effectively sharing our faith from Philip's example? First, he started with questions (8:30), not answers. It's important to understand a person's struggle before we offer a solution. Next, Philip took time to explain what the Bible said about Jesus (8:35). One of the best contexts for that today is a small group Bible study. It's no wonder that many growing churches have an emphasis on small groups.

But the most significant thing about this story is that Philip was willing to take action even when he didn't know why. Philip had no idea what he'd find as he headed for the desert (8:26). He only knew God wanted him to go down that road and be ready. It's really important for anyone who wants to share the Good News – or, for that matter, accomplish anything of value for God – to be willing to listen and obey no matter what. Is God nudging you to do something that doesn't fully make sense?

APPLY   How do you feel about sharing your faith? How might God be at work in the lives of your unbelieving friends? How could you have a part in what God is doing?

PRAY   Father, I know you are at work all around me. Please open my eyes to what you're doing and give me the courage to respond to your prompting.

75   The rainbow coalition

Date: _____   *The Church is born*

PRAY   Father God, show me more about your Son Jesus today.

READ   Acts 10:1–11:18

REFLECT

We've come to a major turning point in our journey through the 'big story' of the Bible. As we've seen, God's plan of salvation began with Abraham (Genesis 12:1–9) and was primarily linked to the history of the Jewish people. Now the circle widens to include non-Jews as well (11:18). It might seem odd that this particular part of the story, the inclusion of the non-Jews, got so much coverage in Acts. But perhaps it underlines what a huge barrier there was between Jews and Gentiles in those days, and therefore what a massive step it was.

The passage also emphasises the active intervention of God in human events (10:3,17,19). Some people think of God as a clock-maker and the world as his clock. They think he made it, wound it up and then had nothing more to do with it. But the Bible teaches not only that God created the world, but also he takes a hands-on approach to what happens in it. At key points, like here, God steps in to guide events according to his loving plan. He does the same in the lives of individual people too. Perhaps you can look back on the events of your life and see some kind of God-created pattern.

The overriding result of this meeting between Peter and Cornelius was to clarify a fundamental truth about God's Good News: salvation through Jesus Christ is for everyone, not just a select group of insiders. The kingdom of heaven is the ultimate 'rainbow coalition'. That's not to say entrance for everyone is automatic. It's open to all who believe in Jesus Christ (10:43) and who therefore receive the Holy Spirit (10:47). Our challenge today is to keep the Church as inclusive as God intended it to be.

APPLY   Are there people in your world who seem outside the reach of the gospel? What could you do to build a bridge between them and the Good News?

PRAY   Forgive me Lord, for keeping your Good News to myself. I'm ready and willing to share it with anyone you want me to.

THE CHURCH IS BORN: REVIEW

From the five readings in this section, summarise any significant insights and any thoughts on applying them to your life.

1

_____

_____

_____

2

_____

_____

_____

3

_____

_____

_____

4

_____

_____

_____

5

_____

_____

_____

Before you begin each new section you may find it helpful to read through your previous Review pages as a reminder of what God has been teaching you.

THE TRAVELS OF PAUL

As we discovered in our last set of readings, the Book of Acts tells the story of how the Good News spread around the world after Jesus ascended into heaven. It's one of the fastest-paced, most exciting books in the Bible. Our readings only cover the highlights, but you'll find reading the whole book is well worth it.

The key player in Acts is Paul, who described himself as 'the least of the apostles' (1 Corinthians 15:9). His Jewish name was Saul and he was one of the 'young guns' among the Pharisees, who were a very traditional and devout group of Jewish leaders. At the same time, Paul was a Roman citizen by birth (Paul was his Roman name), which gave him a considerable amount of freedom and privilege in society at the time. As you will see, God dramatically intervened in Paul's life and used these two aspects of his background to make him the most effective missionary the world has ever known.

Our next five readings will follow Paul on his 'missionary journeys'. Many Bibles have maps in the back that trace these journeys. Take a minute to check them out if you can. You'll see that Paul covered a lot of ground, mostly on foot. He also had to endure all kinds of trouble. Listen to how Paul described the things he went through:

I have worked much harder, been in prison more frequently, been flogged more severely, and been exposed to death again and again. Five times I received from the Jews the forty lashes minus one. Three times I was beaten with rods, once I was stoned, three times I was shipwrecked, I spent a night and a day in the open sea, I have been constantly on the move. I have been in danger from rivers, in danger from bandits, in danger from my own countrymen, in danger from Gentiles; in danger in the city, in danger in the country, in danger at sea; and in danger from false brothers. I have laboured and toiled and have often gone without sleep; I have known hunger and thirst and have often gone without food; I have been cold and naked. Besides everything else, I face daily the pressure of my concern for all the churches (2 Corinthians 11:23–28).

Why did Paul endure all that? It was for two reasons. First, Paul had a real encounter with Jesus. And he realised right away that if Jesus Christ was alive, it was the only thing that really mattered. But, secondly, Paul was God's 'chosen instrument' to share the gospel and plant the Church throughout the known world.

The great American evangelist Dwight L Moody once said, 'The world has yet to see what God could do with one man wholly dedicated to himself'. That may be true. But if anyone has come close, it was Paul, as you are about to see.

76   The only question that matters

Date: _____

PRAY   Lord, I believe your word is 'living and active' and I'm ready to receive it into my soul and spirit today (Hebrews 4:12).

READ   Acts 9:1–31

REFLECT

This passage describes one of the most dramatic transformation stories in the entire Bible. Literally in a flash (9:3), Saul goes from 'breathing out murderous threats against the Lord's disciples' (9:1), to 'proving that Jesus is the Christ' (9:22). How could a person make such a complete turn-around?

The main reason is that God chose him (9:15). Just as God called Abraham centuries earlier (Genesis 12:1–3), he now gives Saul a special assignment. It reminds us that no one is outside of God's reach. He can use the most unlikely people for his glory. It also reminds us to be ready for God's call. He may have a special assignment for you.

A second reason is that Saul had an encounter with Jesus (9:3–6). It's sad, but people can spend a lifetime involved in religious activities yet never understand the truth about Jesus. But on that dusty road, Saul finally got the point: if Jesus is alive, everything changes. The Good News has a way of forcing a person's hand. Once you really understand who Jesus is (9:5) it changes your assumptions, your direction, your friends, your goals; it changes your life forever. As you will see, Saul was transformed into the apostle Paul and spent the rest of his life building the Church.

Another reason for Saul's turnaround was the help of other believers. Ananias had the courage to accept him (9:17) and Barnabas had the wisdom to help him grow in his faith (9:27). Too often Christians are judgemental about the 'rough edges' of new believers, but that criticism can make them vulnerable to falling away.

Perhaps the final reason for Saul's turnaround was his willingness to respond to Jesus. When Saul was knocked off his horse, he asked, 'Lord, what do you want me to do?' (9:6 NKJV). Once we really understand the truth about Jesus, that's the only question that matters.

APPLY   How has meeting Jesus changed your life? What special assignment might he be calling you to now?

PRAY   Lord Jesus, the fact that you want to have a personal relationship with me fills me with joy. If you have a special assignment for me, I'm ready.

77   Sharing Jesus

Date: _____   *The travels of Paul*

PRAY   God, I am eager for a closer walk with you. Show me how I can take another step towards you as I reflect on your Word today.

READ   Acts 13,14

REFLECT

For many years, I was involved in visiting prisons. We organised evangelistic events and Bible studies for inmates. Sometimes this made the prison staff nervous. 'You can have services for those who are already Christians,' they'd tell us. 'But we don't allow *proselytising*.' That's a big offence in our contemporary world. But, as we see in our reading today, God commissioned Barnabas and Saul to do just that (13:2; also see Matthew 28:18–20). You can call it whatever you want, but sharing the Good News with others is the mission of the Church.

Even so, that doesn't give us the right to jam the gospel down a person's throat. Notice the diplomacy Paul used throughout his message (13:16–43). He didn't back away from the hard truths of the gospel, but he presented them in a way that was respectful of his mixed audience (13:26) and which emphasised the positive (13:32,38,39). That combination gets results (13:42–44).

It also stirs up trouble. Throughout this exciting missionary journey, we see a combination of incredible results and vicious opposition. Paul and Barnabas were stealing 'market share' from these religious leaders and they were jealous (13:45). But there was a deeper reason for the opposition (14:2). Becoming a Christian doesn't make a person close-minded – refusing to look at the truth does.

But there were two other factors that made Paul such an effective witness. The first was courage (14:19,20). You may never have to face an angry mob for your faith, but you probably will have to take a risk for it. And when you do, not only will others hear the Good News, but also you'll gain a deeper relationship with God yourself. The second factor was accountability. Paul was sent out by the Church and he reported back to them (13:1–3; 14:26–28). The purpose of evangelism is to build Christ's Church, not our reputations.

APPLY   What risk is God asking you to take in order to share the Good News with others?

PRAY   Lord, I don't feel like a very good 'missionary' but I'm willing to share the Good News with others. Please give me the courage to take a risk for you today.

78   Who is the Church for?

Date: _____

PRAY   Father, I'm so thankful that I can come into your presence because of my belief in what Jesus did in his death and resurrection.

READ   Acts 15

REFLECT

Early in his career, Bill Hybels was forced to quit his position as youth pastor because the elders of the church felt he was attracting 'the wrong kind of kids' to the youth group. Frustrated, Hybels started Willow Creek Community Church, which he intentionally designed to attract non-believers. It became one of the largest churches in America.

Our passage today raises the same question that Bill Hybels asked as a youth pastor: Who is the Church for? In the first century, many thought it was for the Jewish people (15:1), or at least for those who adopted the Jewish customs. But the early Christians needed to understand that the key to God's plan of salvation wasn't race. It was grace (15:11). Of course, the Church is a place for Christians to grow in their faith. But if it ever stops attracting 'the wrong kind of people', it has lost touch with God's vision.

Another fascinating angle to this passage is how the early Church handled a divisive issue. Notice that when the disagreement became public (15:2) the opponents didn't revert to gossip or infighting. Instead, they came together (15:2–4), listened to all sides (15:5–12), remained sensitive to the work of the Holy Spirit (15:8) and, finally, accepted the decision of the leader (15:19). It's a model the Church today would do well to follow.

The chapter ends with a sad but realistic postscript. After risking their lives together for the gospel and avoiding a major split in the emerging Church, Paul and Barnabas couldn't agree on a personnel issue so they parted company (15:37–39; 13:13). Disagreements among Christians happen and when they do we should seek God's wisdom and the counsel of others to avoid unnecessary division. But even when that isn't possible, God can bring good out of our failings. In this case, the disagreement doubled the missionary effort (15:39–41).

APPLY   What kind of people does your church attract? Why? Do you have a disagreement with another group of Christians? How does this passage instruct you?

PRAY   Holy Spirit, I ask for your guidance to know when I should stand up for what I believe and when I should compromise to avoid division.

79
Knowing God's will

Date: _____

PRAY   Thank You, Lord, for the example of Paul. May I be as sold out to you as he was.

READ   Acts 16–20

REFLECT

'Will God punish me if I don't manage to work out what he wants me to do? What if I try, but get it wrong?' Maybe you've felt like that before making a big decision. No doubt Paul was searching for God's direction at the beginning of this new missionary journey. How can we know God's will?

The starting point is waiting on the Lord (13:2,3). It might come more naturally to us to chart our own course and then ask God to bless it. But that can get us into trouble. It's far better to pray, fast, seek advice and wait for the Holy Spirit to guide us. That doesn't mean we need to be frozen into inaction. Notice that Paul seemed to misunderstand God's will at first. He tried to go to Asia, then to Bythinia, and both times God stopped him (16:6,9,10). Finally, God opened the door to Macedonia. When we have taken time to earnestly seek God's will, we can step out in faith even if the way still seems unclear. God can use our detours to get us where he wants us.

But the road won't always be easy. Just think of all the bad things that happened to Paul and his companions in each of these cities. 'Lord, I thought *you* told me to go to Macedonia.' The curious thing is that often God's work does not *look* successful. That's because he uses our weaknesses to accomplish his purposes (2 Corinthians 12:9,10). But no matter what happened – good or bad – Paul stayed focused on the right motivation for ministry (20:24), and so should we.

Paul used different strategies depending on who he was trying to reach. With those who were familiar with the Bible, he 'reasoned from the Scriptures' (17:2). But with those who weren't familiar, he used art and culture to build bridges for sharing the Good News (18:1–17). That's an important model for anyone trying to communicate the gospel in a postmodern world.

APPLY   How do you seek God's will? Has God ever used a detour in your life to accomplish his agenda for you or others?

PRAY   Heavenly Father, when I look back on my life, I can see how you've been guiding me all along. If there is a new direction you want me to take, I ask that you give me the courage to step out in faith.

80

Date: _____

PRAY   Lord, the most important part of my day is spending this time with you. You have the full attention of my mind, my heart and my emotions.

READ   Acts 25–28

REFLECT

What a great story! Conflicting passions, secret plots, political tensions, a dramatic shipwreck – plus an ending that sets the stage for a sequel. Sounds like a thriller, and it is. The Book of Acts is one of the best reads in the Bible.

On the surface it seemed like events were out of control, that Paul's last-ditch appeal to Caesar (25:11) had shipwrecked his ministry. But underneath the apparent disaster, God had a plan, like the strong current beneath choppy waters. He wanted Paul to preach the gospel in the world's most powerful city and he gets him there courtesy of the Roman authorities. If you are experiencing some kind of disaster right now, you may want to ask God to open your eyes to his underlying agenda. 'Lord, what are you trying to say to me through this difficult situation?'

In the midst of seeming chaos, there are two things that kept Paul going. The first was his single-minded focus on the mission God had given him (9:15). Even under the pressure of the confrontation with King Agrippa, Paul never blinked (26:20,28,29). He didn't care if people thought he was crazy. All he cared about was sharing the Good News. You can become an incredibly powerful witness when you stop worrying about what people think about you. The second thing that kept Paul going was the intervention of the Holy Spirit. Several times along the way, God miraculously changed the course of events (27:33,34,44; 28:1–10). When you find yourself in a situation where the only way forward is to trust God, you'll begin to experience more of the Holy Spirit's power in your life.

In the end, it seemed like the result of Paul's ministry was inconclusive. But the truth is, he accomplished exactly what God wanted him to do – to preach the gospel to the Gentiles and the Jews and to plant the Church of Jesus Christ in the major cities of the known world. Well done, good and faithful servant!

APPLY   What mission has God given you? What would it mean for you to trust him in this situation?

PRAY   Dear Lord, Paul is such an inspiration. I'm ready to accept any mission you want to give me and I ask for the Holy Spirit's help to accomplish it.

THE TRAVELS OF PAUL: REVIEW

From the five readings in this section, summarise any significant insights and any thoughts on applying them to your life.

1

_____

_____

_____

2

_____

_____

_____

3

_____

_____

_____

4

_____

_____

_____

5

_____

_____

_____

Before you begin each new section you may find it helpful to read through your previous Review pages as a reminder of what God has been teaching you.

PAUL TO THE CHURCHES

As we discovered in our readings through the Book of Acts, Paul travelled all over the Roman Empire preaching the gospel and starting churches. It was an exciting and dangerous mission and in spite of all the difficulties he encountered, he was effective.

But his church-planting success created a problem. How could he keep these communities of new believers going in the right direction after he was gone? Most of them were living in pagan cities, complete with idolatry and immorality. Often Paul only had time to preach the very basics of the Good News before his enemies ran him out of town. There was so much more he needed to communicate about the gospel, Christian living, the Church and much more.

In addition to his enemies, Paul had to contend with false teachers who were roaming around confusing people by trying to discredit Paul and his ministry. And, on top of all this, Paul was often in prison so he couldn't do anything even if he wanted to. It must have been incredibly frustrating and worrisome to see his life's work eroding before his very eyes. But that's why he was such a passionate letter writer. In addition to prayer, letter writing was key to his strategy for strengthening and building the Church.

In our next readings we'll cover portions from Paul's letters to five different cities – Rome, Galatia, Ephesus, Philippi and Colosse. Each letter contains different advice and comment appropriate to the particular needs in that place. But there are also some strong common themes running through the letters, such as what the unchanging Good News of Jesus is.

As you read Paul's letters you may want to ask yourself: What could I do to strengthen and encourage the Christians around me? In some ways the circumstances Paul was addressing were very different from today. But in other ways they are surprisingly similar. Ask God to show you how you can join Paul in his mission to build the Church.

81

Amen, brother!

Date: _____

PRAY Father, thank you for sending your Son to die for me and your Holy Spirit to live in me. I want these facts to be the most important influences in my life.

READ Romans 8

REFLECT

This chapter reminds me of the sermons of Dr Martin Luther King. It starts slowly and methodically, but as it builds a case it gradually picks up steam and by the end Paul has us on our feet shouting, 'Amen!' For a creative way to understand this passage, try reading it aloud, imagining that you are preaching to a large crowd.

Paul begins his 'sermon' with the basics of the gospel: that Jesus Christ overcame sin and death and then gave us a new Spirit (8:1–4). But it's not good enough just to understand the gospel; we must allow it to affect our actions. Paul goes on to remind us there is no middle ground; either we are controlled by our sinful nature, or we are controlled by the Holy Spirit (8:5–17). If you find yourself struggling to live as a Christian, maybe you haven't clearly made a decision about the controlling influence in your life.

Not that making that choice is always easy. Life is complicated and many situations are ambiguous. But the Holy Spirit can guide us through even when we don't know what to pray for. I sometimes apply Romans 8:26 literally. When I'm overwhelmed, I'll pray, 'Holy Spirit, I don't know what the answer is, but would you pray for … ' and then I identify the situation or perhaps repeat a person's name several times and wait in stillness. Often I sense God's power more than if I came up with a 'solution' to tell God about.

Romans 8:28 is one of those Bible verses you definitely should memorise. But note that it doesn't say everything in your life will be good, fun or successful. That wasn't Paul's experience (8:18,35). But God will *use* everything – even bad things – for your ultimate good, if you belong to him. Being a Christian won't make your life easy, but it will give you the assurance that God really loves you and is in charge or your life. That's what makes you more than a conqueror (8:37).

APPLY What are the controlling influences in your life? What would it mean for you to be controlled by the Spirit?

PRAY Holy Spirit, there are so many situations in my life and in this world that I have no answer for. But I know you are in charge. So here are a few things I ask you to pray about for me…

82

Date: _____

Two lists

PRAY   Lord God, your Word is such an incredible gift. Where else
can I go to find out what you are like and how you want
me to live? Please help me to hear what you want to say to
me today.

READ   Galatians 5:16–6:10

REFLECT

Today, people are uncomfortable with 'absolute truth' – the idea that some
things are always right and other things are always wrong. For them, truth
is more like personal preference. 'What's true for you may not be true for
me. Whatever!'

That wasn't Paul's worldview. For him, there was a sharp contrast between
right and wrong, between good and evil, as we see in this passage. He begins
with a clear picture of the sinful nature (5:19–21). Don't skip over the list
too fast. Although it contains some sins that we're usually careful to avoid
(idolatry, witchcraft), it also contains others that may hit closer to home
(jealousy, envy, selfish ambition). Ironically, the list sounds like a plot
summary of many current films and TV programmes. But Paul's message is
that the sinful nature is no joke, and it has serious consequences (5:21).

In contrast, Paul offers a second list, which he calls the 'fruit of the Spirit'
(5:22,23). These are the qualities we should cultivate in our lives. It takes
work and time, but faithful effort to grow in godliness eventually pays off.
This list also gives us a way to think about God's will. When you have a
choice between two seemingly worthy options, ask yourself: 'With which
option am I most likely to develop more fruit of the Spirit?' That's a good
direction to go in.

But removing the weeds and cultivating the fruit in our lives is tough work,
so Paul suggests two sources of help. The first is fellow believers (6:1–5).
Even when we know the difference between right and wrong, we still make
mistakes. That's when we need Christian friends who can help restore the
broken parts of our lives. The second is the Holy Spirit. Some people are
hesitant about the Holy Spirit. Not Paul. He tells us to 'live by the Spirit'
(5:16), to be 'led by the Spirit' (5:18) and to 'keep in step with the Spirit'
(5:25). The Holy Spirit is God's help for us today.

APPLY   Can you identify any weeds you'd like to remove from
your life? What fruit would you like to cultivate?

PRAY   Holy Spirit, I want to be led by you and keep in step with
you throughout this day, and always.

83

The fight of your life

Date: _____   *Paul to the churches*

PRAY   Lord, I praise you for who you are and I thank you for what
               you've done in my life. Open my eyes to what you want to
               teach me today.

READ   Ephesians 6:10–20

REFLECT

Why do people 'celebrate' Hallowe'en? In a society that is keen to eliminate religious symbols from public places and public events, why do we
spend weeks every autumn displaying symbols that many Christians and
others find offensive – witches, goblins, devils and so on? What's so good
about evil?

Paul was very aware of the reality of evil. And before we can understand
what he had in mind when he described the 'armour of God', we have to
come to grips with why we need it in the first place. Life on earth really is
a spiritual battle. The devil is real; he opposes God and he is scheming
against God's children (6:11,12). It's worth reflecting on the nature of
those schemes. Sometimes they take the form of activities that are obviously evil – like occult practices, substance abuse or promiscuity. Or they
are more subtle – like pride, greed or envy. Either way, the devil uses these
things to destroy what God wants to do in our lives.

That's why we need protection. The way we get it is to protect ourselves
with God's armour – truth, righteousness, the gospel, faith, salvation,
God's Word and prayer (6:14–18). Those aren't just comforting words.
They are the weapons God has given us to survive in the spiritual battle.

Notice that Paul encourages his readers to be proactive. 'Be strong ... stand
your ground ... stand firm ... be alert ... pray in the Spirit.' No matter who
you are, no matter how long you've been a Christian, you can expect to
face the devil's attacks. The apostle Peter was even more direct. He said
Satan was like a lion, looking for someone to devour (1 Peter 5:8). The best
defence against evil is to put on the full armour of God.

APPLY   How have you been aware that you are in a spiritual battle?
               What are you doing to put on God's armour?

PRAY   Lord, I'm not afraid because I know you have already won
               the battle and I belong to you. But, I don't want to become
               complacent, so I ask for your help to put on your armour
               for whatever battle you call me to.

84 Give peace a chance

Date: _____

Paul to the churches

PRAY   Father, my life is so stressful and discouraging at times. I would love to experience more of your peace and joy today.

READ   Philippians 4:2–9

REFLECT

It's interesting that Paul wrote this famous section about God's peace at a time when he was in prison (1:12-14,17) and there was interpersonal tension in the church (4:2–3). We can experience peace not only when everything is smooth, but also in the midst of the problems of life. So how exactly does Paul say that we can do that? It requires at least three conscious decisions.

Rejoice The first is the decision to rejoice – whether you feel like it or not (4:4). That's because the focus of our rejoicing is the Lord, not our circumstances. We praise God for who he is, not for what may be happening to us at the moment. I once attended a meeting where several Christians gathered to discuss some very stressful issues that threatened to divide the group. I noticed one of my friends seemed especially happy. When I asked why, he said that at the break he had walked around the perimeter of the car park in the dark, praising the Lord. He was rejoicing in the midst of the tension.

Pray The second decision is to pray (4:6). Sometimes we become so overwhelmed by our worries that we can't sleep. If you find yourself lying in bed imagining worst-case scenarios for your life, get up and pray. I find it helpful to get on my knees and pour out my worries to God. Then, still on my knees, I raise my hands as high as I can and praise the Lord. I've found these middle of the night 'prayer meetings' are the times when I most experience the peace that 'transcends all understanding'. And I'm usually able to go right back to sleep too!

Be positive The third decision is to focus on positive things (4:9). Sometimes we have so many problems that they 'fill the screen' of our minds. That's when we need to click the 'minimise button' on our worries and open some new screens that remind us of God's goodness. Rejoice, pray, minimise. That's the way to exchange anxiety for peace.

APPLY   Make a list of the things that are worrying you today. Now, make a list of the things for which you can praise God.

PRAY   Lord, I give my worries and anxieties to you, even though you already know what they are. And I rejoice because you have a plan for my life and nothing can separate me from your love.

85   What about the drifters?

Date: _____   *Paul to the churches*

PRAY   Lord God, I ask that you would fill me with the knowledge of your will, that I may bear fruit and live a life that pleases you.

READ   Colossians 1:1–23

REFLECT

Perhaps you have a friend or family member who was once very committed to being a Christian, but over the years their enthusiasm has waned to the point where that commitment is questionable. How can we encourage Christians who are drifting away from their faith? That was the challenge the apostle Paul was facing when he wrote this letter to the Colossians.

Paul started by emphasising the positive (1:3–6). Growing in Christ doesn't always follow a straight line. Sometimes an initial commitment is followed by a setback. Instead of scolding the Colossians, Paul praised their good start and reminded them of their positive influence on others. He also assured them of his prayers (1:9–14). New believers need encouragement and prayer, not criticism.

But the Colossians *were* in danger of getting off track by adding things to the gospel. Some thought they had to follow Jewish rules to be a Christian. Others thought they had to obtain secret knowledge to be a Christian. Paul corrected these misunderstandings by going back to the heart of the gospel: Jesus Christ. He chose every phrase of his carefully worded statement (1:15–20) to communicate the important truths about Jesus. Now they were ready to hear the Good News, and Paul gave it to them in concentrated form (1:21–23).

Paul's strategy for helping the Colossians provides a good example for us. Too often we expect perfection in new believers and criticise them as soon as they fall. 'See, I knew he wasn't genuine.' We need to pray for anyone who may have drifted from the faith, that they would get re-focused on Jesus Christ, while recognising that God knows what's in a person's heart – not us.

APPLY   Do you know some 'drifters'? What could you do to encourage them in their faith this week? How could you help re-focus them on Jesus Christ?

PRAY   Jesus, thank you for reconciling me to God. Keep me close.

PAUL TO THE CHURCHES: REVIEW

From the five readings in this section, summarise any significant insights and any thoughts on applying them to your life.

1

_____

_____

_____

2

_____

_____

_____

3

_____

_____

_____

4

_____

_____

_____

5

_____

_____

_____

Before you begin each new section you may find it helpful to read through your previous Review pages as a reminder of what God has been teaching you.

PAUL TO THE LEADERS

According to author J Robert Clinton, 'Leadership is a dynamic process in which a man or woman with God-given capacity influences a specific group of God's people towards his purposes for the group', (*The Making of a Leader*, Navpress, 1988). One of the most important tasks of a Christian leader is preparing and empowering new leaders. In fact, the best way for Christian leaders to test whether they have lasting influence is to ask whether they are able to leave their ministry – whether it is a large organisation or a small Sunday school class – in capable hands.

After many years of preaching the gospel and planting churches, Paul's active ministry was nearing an end (2 Timothy 4:6,7). He realised that finding the next generation of leaders for the Church was his final challenge. He even summarised his leadership development strategy in a letter to his protégé Timothy: 'And the things you have heard me say in the presence of many witnesses entrust to reliable men who will also be qualified to teach others' (2 Timothy 2:2). For Paul, the future of the Church was all about finding good people.

In our next five readings, we see Paul writing to train and encourage the leaders of the early Church, primarily Timothy. He provides a job description for church leaders, warns against the pitfalls of leadership, clarifies some key issues and stresses the importance of two fundamentals of Christian leadership: the gospel and God's Word.

These readings also give us some insight into the stresses of the first century Church. For one thing, it was growing in spite of persecution. As we saw in the Book of Acts, God sometimes uses persecution to grow his kingdom. But the Church was also encountering internal strife in the form of false teachers. And of these two stresses, it is clear that Paul saw the latter as the more serious threat to the growth of the Church. It still is. Paul confronts these twin challenges with a combination of encouragement and correction for leaders.

Maybe you don't think of yourself as a leader. But if you reflect on the definition of Christian leadership above, you may want to reconsider. Everyone, including you, can influence others for God's purposes. If that's true, the apostle Paul has some good advice for you, as you are about to discover.

86 The habits of highly effective leaders

Date: _____

Paul to the leaders

PRAY   Lord, I want to grow in my walk with you. I'm ready to be shaped by your Word today.

READ   1 Timothy 3

REFLECT

Success creates problems. That's what Paul was feeling as he wrote this letter to his protégé, Timothy. In spite of opposition and hardships, Paul's missionary journeys were incredibly successful. Churches were popping up all over the place. But the problem was, who was going to lead them?

Anyone who's been part of a growing organisation knows that good leadership is essential. Jesus understood this and made hands-on leadership training one of his highest priorities (Luke 6:12–16; 9:1–6; 10:1–17). Now Paul faced the same challenge; if his church-planting success was to last beyond his lifetime, he had to find a new generation of leaders. The question was, how?

Paul started with 'job descriptions' that set high standards (3:2–13). And whether you think of yourself as a leader in your church or not, these are good goals to work on. Notice that the lists balance personal traits, family issues and a good outside reputation. A Christian leader is a well-rounded person, not just a good talker.

Sometimes today people act as if the leaders are the most important part of the Church. In so doing, they lose sight of a more important principle. The Church doesn't belong to its leaders, it belongs to God (3:15). He's the boss. Leaders serve him by serving others. Anyone who aspires to leadership in the Church must add one more quality to the list: humility.

But the fact remains that if the Church is going to grow, quality leadership is the biggest need. That doesn't mean you need to be the world's greatest preacher or church-planter. The Church needs solid leadership at every level – Sunday School teachers, outreach programme leaders, home group leaders and more. If that's so, perhaps you should begin developing your leadership qualities right away. God may be calling you soon.

APPLY   What could you do to develop your leadership abilities? How could you begin to use these abilities in your church?

PRAY   Lord, you know I'm still growing in many areas. But I'm willing to use the abilities you've given me in your Church. If you call me to leadership, I'll follow.

87

Show me the money

Date: _____

PRAY   Lord Jesus, you have offered me a 'pearl of great price'
(Matthew 13:44–46). I value my relationship with you
more than anything else.

READ   1 Timothy 6:3–21

REFLECT

I once heard a prisoner describe the goal of his life before he went to jail:
'All I wanted was lots more of them lovely tenners and twenties'. We may
not be as candid about our interest in money, but the truth is, it has a powerful influence in our lives. Paul knew this, so he made a special point in
his letter to Timothy of explaining at least three important 'financial prin-
ciples' for Christians.

Loving money leads to evil (6:10) Having money isn't evil; loving it is. But
what does it mean to 'love' money? When we love a person, we think
about them all the time, make decisions with them in mind, devote a lot
of our time to them. Does that describe your relationship with money? If
it does, watch out.

Greed leads to strife (6:3–5) You can tell money has become too important
when it infects other areas of our lives. In the early Church, the greed of
some leaders weakened their commitment to sound teaching, which produced envy, strife, malicious talk, evil suspicions and constant friction.
Even today, money is at the bottom of many church squabbles.

Godliness leads to contentment (6:6) Some people think that having lots of
money will make them happy. But often it only makes them hungry for
more. John D Rockefeller, one of the richest men in the world, was once
asked, 'How much is enough?' He answered, 'Just a little bit more'. The
secret of happiness is not to pursue more money; it is to pursue the goals
and values of God's kingdom and then to let the chips fall where they may
(Matthew 6:33).

But we should be careful not to conclude that just because money and possessions have a powerful influence, they are all bad. Paul acknowledged
that some Christians will be rich (6:17). Still, he commanded them to
make God their first priority, to do good deeds and share their resources.
That's a challenge we in the West need to accept.

APPLY   It is often said you can tell a lot about a person by examining
their cheque book. What does yours say about you?

PRAY   Lord, thank you for the ways you bless me with material
things. Please help me to have more passion for serving
you than spending money.

88

Date: _____

PRAY   Lord, there are times in my life when I get tired and worn out, both physically and spiritually. Please renew my passion to know you and my desire to serve you as I read your Word today.

READ   2 Timothy 2

REFLECT

Mentoring has become a big deal these days. Researchers have found that mentoring makes a positive impact in the lives of troubled young people. It also helps employees from minority groups to be more successful in a large corporation.

In this passage, we see Paul acting as a 'spiritual mentor' to Timothy. Paul was keenly aware of Timothy's conversion and was instrumental in helping him discover his spiritual gift (1:5,6). Now Paul is writing to coach Timothy on how to be an effective leader in the emerging Church. If you find yourself eager for a spiritual mentor, try reading 1 and 2 Timothy as if Paul were writing just to you.

Paul uses four images to help Timothy understand his ministry (2:3–7,15). The thing that a soldier, an athlete, a farmer and a workman all have in common is their focus on the task. If they get distracted, they will fail to accomplish their objective. That was Paul's message to Timothy and to you: no matter how difficult things get, stay focused on the mission of living and sharing the gospel.

It's interesting that although Paul mentions several potential distractions including the blanket term 'evil desires of youth' (2:22), the one he seems most concerned about here is arguing (2:14–26). Some Christian leaders today seem more interested in arguing with each other about non-essential issues than sharing the gospel and God's Word with a needy world. If Paul were here today, he'd say, 'Cut it out! You're getting distracted'. Even Christian leaders need a mentor.

APPLY   Think of some people who are older and wiser in their faith and life experience. Is there one who would make a good spiritual mentor for you? How could you approach them about this?

PRAY   Lord God, forgive me for the ways I allow myself to become distracted. With your help, I want to be a focused and effective witness for you.

89   **Finishing well**

Date: _____   *Paul to the leaders*

PRAY   Lord God, thank you for the gift of your Word. Help me to live it out today.

READ   2 Timothy 3:10–4:5

REFLECT

Psychologists talk about 'door knob statements'. These are the throwaway comments a patient makes as he or she lingers at the door before leaving a counselling session. They usually reveal the main thing on their mind. This passage is like a long 'door knob statement' from Paul. He knows he's about to leave this world (4:6) and these verses are his parting thoughts to Timothy before he dies. What were the last things Paul wanted to emphasise?

Suffering The first had to do with suffering (3:12). Paul says suffering is inevitable not just for evangelists and church-planters, but for 'everyone who wants to live a godly life'. It's the one Bible promise you'll never find on a bookmark or poster. That doesn't mean we should go looking for trials and troubles. But we shouldn't be shocked when they come. In fact, God will use them to help us grow (James 1:2–4; 1 Peter 1:6,7).

Scripture The second thing Paul emphasised was Scripture (3:15,16). If Jesus Christ is the cornerstone of the Church (1 Peter 2:4–10), the Bible is the plumb line for keeping it in line with God's priorities and values (Amos 7:7,8). Paul stresses that the Bible is like no other book because it expresses the words of God ('God-breathed') and it therefore has at least three purposes: *to explain* God's plan of salvation, *to train* us for godly living and *to motivate* us for good works. Are those the outcomes of your Bible reading?

Mission Finally, Paul challenges Timothy to continue his mission of preaching the word (4:1,2). It's interesting to read how Paul summed up his own experiences and mission in life (3:10,11). How would you sum up yours? In spite of all the things that happened to Paul along the way, he had the joy of knowing that he was finishing well (4:7,8).

APPLY   How would you describe your mission for the rest of your life? What will it take for you to finish well?

PRAY   Father, I want to commit the rest of my life to pursuing the goals that matter most to you.

90

I want to be ready

Date: _____

Paul to the leaders

PRAY   If you can, go outside or to a window and look up into the sky. Pray aloud offering God thanksgiving and praise.

READ   1 Thessalonians 4:13–5:11

REFLECT

One issue that caused confusion for leaders in the early Church was the Second Coming of Christ. Most believers were aware that Jesus said he was coming back, but when? Some thought it would be in a matter of days, so they gave up work. Others claimed he had already returned. The Church needed some clear teaching on this slippery issue.

Occasionally today we hear of a group that has sold all their goods and gone to a mountaintop to wait for the Second Coming at a time they believe they have identified. Or a Bible teacher who claims to have figured out the date of Christ's return. No doubt such people are motivated by an intense and admirable devotion to Christ. But they've lost sight of what the Bible says about the subject.

Just because some people misunderstand the Second Coming doesn't mean we should avoid the topic altogether. Paul didn't hesitate to talk about what Christ's return would be like; he said it will be a spectacular event (4:16,17). Jesus himself took time to explain to his followers what it will be like (4:15; Matthew 24). Our challenge today is to neither over-emphasise nor under-emphasise this important fact.

Paul was hesitant to talk about *when* the Second Coming would happen (5:1–3). The main thing we need to know is that it will be a surprise, like 'a thief in the night'. Instead of trying to determine exactly when it will happen, we should focus on being alert and self-controlled (5:6) so that no matter when it does, we'll be ready.

If we can keep that balance, the hope of Christ's return should be one of the most encouraging realities of the Christian life (4:18). Imagine what it will be like to hear the trumpets and the voice of the archangel, and then finally to see the Lord face to face!

APPLY   How does the reality of Christ's return affect the way you live your life? How should it?

PRAY   Lord Jesus, the fact that some day I'll be able to see you face to face blows my mind and fills me with joy. Help me to live this day with that wonderful truth in mind.

PAUL TO THE LEADERS: REVIEW

From the five readings in this section, summarise any significant insights and any thoughts on applying them to your life.

1

_____

_____

_____

2

_____

_____

_____

3

_____

_____

_____

4

_____

_____

_____

5

_____

_____

_____

Before you begin each new section you may find it helpful to read through your previous Review pages as a reminder of what God has been teaching you.

THE APOSTLES' TEACHING

Our next five readings introduce us to the writings of four great leaders of the first century Church.

Although he was not originally one of the 12 disciples, Paul became a believer when he met Jesus on the Damascus road, as we discovered in an earlier section. After that, he became the greatest evangelist and most prolific writer in the entire New Testament. If you want to know what it means to go all out for the gospel, read the letters of Paul.

But in the gospel accounts, Peter was the most prominent disciple. He frequently acted on impulse, which sometimes led to some incredible breakthroughs (Luke 9:20) and other times led to some humiliating failures (Luke 22:54–62). But Jesus restored him and gave him a new mission. The new Peter was the first one to explain the gospel on the day of Pentecost, and the first one to take it to the non-Jews. His lifetime of successes and failures as a follower of Jesus gave him a deep insight into the Christian faith. If you want a clear and passionate expression of the implications of being born again, read the letters of Peter.

In the New Testament, five different people have the name James. But it was most likely James, the brother of Jesus (Matthew 13:55; Mark 6:3) who was the leader of the church in Jerusalem (Acts 15:13–21) and who later wrote the Book of James. Perhaps because of his relationship to Jesus, or perhaps because of his wisdom, he was authoritative, straightforward and direct. If you want to understand the practical implications of the faith, read the letter of James.

Of all the disciples, John had perhaps the closest relationship with Jesus (John 13:23). But it wasn't until John saw the empty tomb that he finally believed Jesus was who he said he was (John 20:8). At the beginning of his life, he was a rough and ready sort of guy. But by the end of his life he had become one of the most thoughtful of all the disciples. If you want to understand the deep implications of Jesus' love, read the letters of John.

So get ready to dig into the letters of the men who were closest to Jesus. They have a lot to say to you.

91

Date: _____

The active ingredient

PRAY   Lord, so much of this world is devoted to chasing the
illusion of love. But I pray that you will help me know and
experience the reality of your love today.

READ   1 Corinthians 13

REFLECT

I married Carol Capra on June 4, 1977 and she has been one of the greatest blessings that God has brought into my life. But, every once in a while,
we get on each other's nerves! In fact, I am ashamed to admit that there
have been times when our frustration with each other has lasted several
days. When that happens, I've discovered the best thing to do is get by
myself and prayerfully read this chapter. I've been amazed at how quickly
these words can challenge and melt my hardened heart.

Paul had just finished an extended discussion of spiritual gifts but he called
love 'the most excellent way' (12:31b). That doesn't mean things like
wisdom or faith or healing (12:7–11) are bad. It's just that without love
even the most gifted person has missed the point. Love is the active ingre-
dient of the Christian life.

At the heart of this chapter (13:4–7), Paul answered the question, 'What
is love?' You can read all the literature that's ever been written and not find
a better expression of love than this. It's definitely worth memorising. And
yet, as wonderful as this passage is, it's still only the second best expression of love ever. The best was Jesus Christ's death on the cross for the sins
of the world.

When you think about it, we spend so much of our lives pursuing things
that are temporary or just plain worthless. This passage reminds us that
the things in life that have the greatest value are faith, hope and love. But
love is the greatest. And the best way to find it is to give it away.

APPLY   In what ways are you pursuing faith, hope and love in your
life? How could you live out Paul's definition of love this
week?

PRAY   Thank you, Jesus, for your incredible love for me. With
your help, I intend to share that love with the people in
my world through my words, attitudes and actions.

92

Date: _____

The apostles' teaching

PRAY   Father, show me just a little bit more what it means to live by faith and not by sight today.

READ   2 Corinthians 4:1–6:2

REFLECT

Clark Kent is a mild-mannered newspaper reporter. But, when evil and danger lurk, he steps out of sight and is transformed into… Superman! After that, the bad guys don't stand a chance. The transformation of that comic book hero gives us just a little picture of what Paul had in mind when he described what it means to be a 'new creation' in Christ (5:17). When we hear and receive the gospel, everything in our lives changes, and the devil doesn't stand a chance.

You'd think a message about new life would be wildly popular. But not always! In this passage, Paul described his efforts to share this 'unpopular' message (4:2,8–12) and in so doing, gave us some incredible insights into the meaning of the gospel.

The first thing he emphasised is *this ministry* (4:1), which he later described as 'a ministry of reconciliation' (5:18). Ever since Adam and Eve sinned in the Garden of Eden, people have been separated from God. That's the 'big problem'. But the 'big story' is that Jesus died on the cross for the sins of the world. The Good News is that through faith in Jesus Christ we can be reunited with God.

No wonder Paul refers to the gospel as *this treasure* (4:7). Amazingly, God chose to place that message in 'jars of clay', that is, weak, faltering people like you, Paul and me. Even so, as a new person, you have a new mission – to be Christ's ambassador (5:20). That makes you a supernatural hero.

APPLY   In what ways have you become a 'new creation' as a result of following Jesus?

PRAY   Lord, forgive me for not feeling or acting like your ambassador. But I ask that you enable me to share the treasure you've given me with others.

93

Sure, I'm sure!

Date: _____

The apostles' teaching

PRAY Lord Jesus, I rejoice because the hope you have offered me is more valuable and lasting than anything this world has to offer.

READ 1 Peter 1:1–2:12

REFLECT

An agnostic is a person who says it isn't possible to know God. For some, this seems intellectually honest – but in fact, it is a hopeless dilemma. The one thing agnostics believe is that it isn't possible to believe. That takes a lot of faith.

Peter was no intellectual but he was very, very sure about what he believed. The reason? He had seen the risen Christ (John 21). When you really think about it, that's the only thing that could explain why a bunch of powerless, uneducated disciples could all of a sudden become fearless evangelists, willing to suffer and sacrifice their lives. If they knew the resurrection wasn't true, they would eventually have backed off. But they couldn't, because they had seen Jesus alive again.

So what was Peter so sure about? The first thing was the *new birth* (1:3). Being free of our sin and reunited with God is like being born again (1:23; John 3:1–21). It's a new life. The second thing is a *living hope* (1:3). Because Jesus is alive, we have real hope, not just fairy tales to help us sleep at night. No matter what happens in this world, you can have the solid assurance that some day you'll be with Jesus forever.

Because of that, we should be 'strangers' to the evil ways of this world (2:11). Instead, we should focus on living self-controlled, loving and holy lives (1:13–16,22), even if we have to suffer or if everything goes wrong. And we can always rejoice because the 'big story' has a happy ending for all who believe in Jesus Christ, and nothing can change that (1:4). In the meantime, we gain strength and support knowing we are part of the Church – not a building, but 'a people belonging to God' (2:9,10) with the living Christ as its leader. The Good News is that Jesus makes hope possible.

APPLY What things make you sure about your faith? What things make you the most hopeful in life? How are your answers demonstrated in your life?

PRAY Lord, may the joy of my salvation and my commitment to follow you with all my heart be evident to everyone I meet.

94

Just do it!

The apostles' teaching

PRAY   Help me today, Lord, as I look intently into your Word. I want to experience the blessing of doing what you say to me.

READ   James 1,2

REFLECT

If Peter was a fighter and Paul was a thinker, James was a doer. And the main focus of his letter is to describe the practical aspects of what it means to be a Christian.

As we have seen, first century Christians were experiencing persecution. James' practical advice was to view these trials not as a reason to complain but an opportunity to grow (1:2–4). He had his finger on an important truth: often the thing that causes us to grow most in our walk with Christ is a time of crisis because, more than anything else, it forces us to depend on God. That doesn't mean you should go looking for trouble. But when it happens, rejoice! God has given you an opportunity to grow.

James also had some practical things to say about speaking. His advice reminds us of the Book of Proverbs, as he suggests we need to be 'quick to listen, slow to speak and slow to become angry' (1;19,26; 3:1–12). What would happen if you spent an entire day trying to listen more than speaking? James also suggested a practical approach to the Word of God: it's good to reflect on it – but it's better to act on it (1:22–25).

Perhaps the most famous quote from this letter is, 'Faith without deeds is dead' (2:26). It would be easy to misunderstand what James meant. It's not that faith is unimportant, or that doing good things is what God cares about most. The Bible is very clear that we can't earn our salvation (Ephesians 2:8,9). What James is saying is that if your faith is real, it must show up in your actions. If you were unable to speak, would others know you were a follower of Jesus?

APPLY   Think of all the things you do which demonstrate the reality of your faith to others. What could you add to the list?

PRAY   Lord God, I'm so thankful for the truth of your Word. Give me a willingness and passion to do what it says.

95   **Authentic Christianity**

Date: _____   *The apostles' teaching*

PRAY   Father, thank you for loving me. Lord Jesus, thank you for saving me. Holy Spirit, thank you for living in me.

READ   1 John 3:11–4:21

REFLECT

'I'm not sure when I became a Christian.' Some people worry too much about that question; others not enough. The important thing is to know you are in Christ *now*. So what are the marks of a true Christian? John offers us three essentials.

The first is to *believe in Jesus Christ* (3:23). That's the foundation of authentic Christian faith. And believing means at least two things: it's *agreeing* that Jesus is who he said he was, the risen Son of God, and then *following* his commands. Once you've decided to take those steps, nothing can separate you from the love of God (Romans 8:31–39).

The second essential of a true Christian is to *receive the Holy Spirit* (4:13). There is a lot of controversy about the work of the Holy Spirit in the Church today. Some want to limit his work, perhaps as a reaction to those who over-emphasise his work. But the New Testament is clear that the Holy Spirit is not something extra or just for a select few. He's here and available to all Jesus' followers (Acts 2:14–21).

The third mark of a true Christian is to *love others* (3:11,23; 4:21). John is blunt on this point (3:15; 4:7,8), but so was Jesus (4:11, 3:23b). And if you want to know what love is, think about what Jesus did. He gave his life for others (3:16). That's the highest standard of love possible. You may not be called on to become a martyr, but John is saying that Christian love involves sacrifice.

John knew what authentic Christianity was all about because he had been with Jesus. And he gave us this eyewitness report so we could have the assurance and joy of knowing him too (1:1–4).

APPLY   When have you ever given or received sacrificial love? Is there evidence of authentic Christianity in your life?

PRAY   Lord Jesus, I believe that you are the living Son of God. Empower me by your Spirit to follow you with my whole heart.

THE APOSTLES' TEACHING: REVIEW

From the five readings in this section, summarise any significant insights and any thoughts on applying them to your life.

1

_____

_____

_____

2

_____

_____

_____

3

_____

_____

_____

4

_____

_____

_____

5

_____

_____

_____

Before you begin each new section you may find it helpful to read through your previous Review pages as a reminder of what God has been teaching you.

REVELATION

Revelation is a challenging book, yet perhaps the most popular and most studied of the prophetic books in the Bible. People sometimes refer to it as The Revelation of St John. But that can be a little misleading because, in fact, it is the revelation of Jesus Christ (1:1). John was simply the recipient who described it for us to read.

From the very beginning, John established that this was a message from God about the future (1:1–3). The way God revealed that message was through a series of seven visions while John was on the island of Patmos (1:9).

The first vision referred to the early Church around AD 81–96. It had been approximately 50 years since Jesus had ascended into heaven and the Church was beginning to drift away from the gospel. Not only were Christians facing persecution, but they were beginning to accept false teaching and adopt sinful patterns of behaviour. You'll find the messages to the seven churches (2:1–3:22) very relevant to today.

The visions about the end of the world that follow on from the messages to the churches are very challenging to understand. Some have tried to figure out the meaning of every detail in these visions. But that can be confusing at best. You might find it more helpful to reflect on the main themes from these visions, the way you do when you try to remember a dream you've had at night.

Probably the biggest theme running through the last chapters of Revelation is the final showdown between good and evil, between God and Satan. The visions give us a picture of how the devil will be defeated and what heaven will be like. Again, our natural curiosity makes us want to get the exact picture of what it will be like. But the truth is, it will be even better than we can imagine. Why? Because the main feature of heaven is that all those who believe in Jesus will be with him forever!

One last thought before you complete your journey through the Bible. Don't let this be the end of your Bible reading experience. Let it become the beginning of a lifetime dialogue with God. Once you've decided to become a follower of Jesus Christ, the best way to sustain and grow your relationship with him is to meet him daily in the Bible and prayer. (If you'd like information on how to receive more Bible reading help, see page 160.) And thanks for walking with me through the **Essential 100**!

96

Date: _____

PRAY   Lord God, I want to worship you in Spirit and truth (John 4:24). As I do, please give me a deeper understanding of Jesus.

READ   Revelation 1

REFLECT

Let's nail down the facts: the apostle John is probably 90 years old by this time, and it's about 50 years since Jesus left the earth. God directed John to go to the island of Patmos (1:9), but he didn't know what would happen next. So he devoted himself to worshipping God (1:10).

That's a good thing to do when you are unsure what to do next in life – in fact, connecting with God in worship is especially good when you don't have all the answers! True worship reminds us that God is present and in charge of every detail in our lives.

Worship also leads to deeper insight. First, John gets a better understanding of Jesus, the central figure in the vision (1:13). Jesus is dazzling and overwhelming and he holds the keys to death and hell (1:18). That's a pretty powerful position. When he came to earth the first time, Jesus came as Saviour. When he comes again, Jesus will come as Judge. A second insight John gets during worship is a better understanding of God's perspective on the Church (1:11). But we'll hear more about that in our next reading.

As you read these verses, you may have thought, 'I wish my relationship with God could be as real and personal as John's'. Notice the clues John gave us about his walk with God. We've already noted that he committed himself to whole-hearted worship. In addition, he was obedient to the Word of God (1:2,9), he was focused on Jesus (1:2–8), he eagerly embraced the Holy Spirit (1:10) and he was enduring suffering (1:9). That's the prescription for a deeper walk with God.

APPLY   How would you describe your relationship with God? How is that seen in the way you worship him?

PRAY   Jesus, you are almighty, the first and the last, the eternally living and present. I worship and praise you from the depths of my heart.

97   Good news, bad news

Date: _____   *Revelation*

PRAY   Lord, the door of my heart is open to you. I want to hear your voice and experience close fellowship with you today.

READ   Revelation 2:1–3:22

REFLECT

One thing stands out in this passage: Jesus really cares about the Church. That's a sobering thought, especially when we think of some of the things that go on in churches today, and the low opinion that many have about them. But Jesus is there and he knows what's going on; notice how many times he said, 'I know… ' (2:2,9,13,19; 3:1,8,15).

So what did Jesus have to say to these seven churches? There are different variations, but the main theme is to contrast congregations who were faithful in teaching and practice with those who were unfaithful. If you have time, make a grid of the seven churches on a sheet of paper. Then, next to each, summarise what they were commended for and what they were criticised for. You'll get a pretty clear picture of what Jesus wants from his people.

Two churches received only praise (Smyrna and Philadelphia). And note what it was for: they were poor and weak (2:9; 3:8). It's a fact that when we are powerless, we are much more willing to depend on God's power. That's the secret of an effective church. Contrast that with the church in Sardis. Their problem was they thought they were alive when in fact they were dead (3:1). Jesus' definition of success is often very different to ours. His message to a successful, dead church: go back to the basics of the gospel – obey and repent (3:3).

In a way, this passage can seem harsh. No church could ever completely measure up to what Jesus wants. But the encouraging thing is that his discipline is a reflection of his love for the church… and for you (3:19; Proverbs 3:12; Hebrews 12:6,10). So take heart, Jesus wants a relationship with you (3:20) and he's willing to go to great lengths to have it (Romans 5:8).

APPLY   How do you think Jesus would feel about your church? What message might he have for your church and for you?

PRAY   Lord Jesus, you are my first love. Forgive me for the times when I become lukewarm in my commitment.

98

Heavens!

Date: _____

Revelation

PRAY   You are worthy, my Lord and my God, to receive glory and honour and power, for you created all things, and by your will they were created and have their being.

READ   Revelation 4:1 – 7:17

REFLECT

This was some dream! Twenty-four elders dressed in white, horses, creatures with wings, a great worshipping multitude and more. You don't need special effects to make this passage come alive. Some have tried to determine exactly what every detail means. But, for our purposes, it's more helpful to look at the big picture: this is a vision of heaven.

What's your picture of heaven? The stereotypical view of heaven is as a place in the clouds where people go after death to strum harps and watch their relatives below. Country music makes it sound like the best thing about heaven is that we get to meet Mother and Dad. Maybe we will, but the best thing by far will be to meet Jesus. The Lamb of God is at the very centre of heaven (5:6; 7:17). Nothing else compares to that.

Yet there are some ominous aspects to John's vision. For example, the way to heaven isn't always a sentimental journey; sometimes it involves suffering (6:9). Also, it seems like things may get worse before they finally get better (chapter 6). But for those who belong to the Lamb, the end becomes the beginning of a wonderful eternity with Jesus (7:15 – 17).

So what will we do in heaven? The Book of Revelation highlights worship as the main activity. What else could you do in the presence of Jesus? And note the make-up of this spectacular worshipping community. 'Every nation, tribe, people and language' (7:9) will be represented. The reason we should share the Good News with all people and welcome them into our churches is not to be politically correct. It's because that's what heaven will be like.

APPLY   Why do you want to go to heaven? If God said to you, 'Why should I let you into heaven?' what would you say?

PRAY   I praise you for saving me, and for giving me heaven to look forward to.

99   **Waiting at the lookout**

Date: _____   *Revelation*

PRAY   Hallelujah! For you, Lord God Almighty, reign over all
creation.

READ   Revelation 19,20

REFLECT

Several years ago, we took a family trip to Niagara Falls on the border
between New York and Canada. Standing on the lookout at the very edge
of the falls, we could see the deep water of the Niagara River as it picked
up speed and went careening over the edge into a roaring chasm far below.
This passage is like standing on a lookout at the end of the world. It
describes the incredible, unstoppable power of God sending Satan and evil
over the edge into the abyss.

Although there are many curious and intriguing details to this passage, the
main point is that in the end, evil will be defeated (19:11–20:10). It
doesn't always look that way now, especially when we see some of the
awful things that happen in our world. At times, the devil may seem to
have the upper hand. But the Bible assures us that he doesn't; he lost the
decisive battle at the cross. What a wonderful thing to know that Satan's
doom is guaranteed!

Another reality of the end is judgement (20:11–15). That's what the 'book
of life' symbolised. Some people envision the final judgement like a big set
of scales. If your good deeds outweigh your bad deeds, you get a ticket to
heaven. But that's not what the Bible says. Only those who believe in Jesus
will be saved (Romans 3:23; 5:8; 10:9).

For those who are in Christ, the end of the world will be a time of joy and
celebration (19:1–10). The image John saw in his vision was that of a mag-
nificent wedding with Jesus (the Lamb) as the groom and the Church as
his bride (19:7). Imagine what it will be like to stand at that lookout at the
end of the world and be taken up to meet Jesus in the air. Hallelujah!

APPLY   Are you ready for the final judgement? Are you certain that
you are in Christ?

PRAY   Jesus, I believe you are my Lord and Saviour and that God
raised you from the dead. I'm waiting for that wonderful
day when you come to take me home.

100

Date: _____

Those pearly gates

PRAY   'Your word, O Lord, is eternal; it stands firm in the heavens' (Psalm 119:89). Thank you so much, Father, for what you have taught me from my journey through the Bible.

READ   Revelation 21,22

REFLECT

When our children were young, we had an illustrated edition of John Bunyan's classic allegory *The Pilgrim's Progress*. It's the story of a man named Christian who takes a journey from the City of Destruction through all kinds of dangers and temptations to the foot of the cross, and finally to heaven. We read it at bedtime so many times that the binding finally wore out. Our children are grown now, but I still love to read that tattered book aloud. And whenever I get to the part where Christian enters the celestial city, I still cry with joy. That's how I feel when I read this passage.

How can you express what it will be like to enter the gates of heaven? These two chapters are filled with what have become popular images of that wonderful moment – pearly gates, streets of gold, river of life, etc. But, as incredible as all that may sound, the reality of heaven is better still in two important ways.

First, *everything will be new* (21:5). Part of the curse of sin was that everything became subject to destruction and death (Romans 8:19–22). But when Jesus returns for his Church, he will create a new heaven and a new earth (21:1), and a new Jerusalem will appear (21:2). Those are powerful images to describe how God will re-create his world. One joy of being a Christian is that you can be sure one day that your body, your life, your world, everything will all become gloriously new.

But the second and most important reality of heaven is that it is the place where *God will dwell with his people forever* (21:3). That was his plan from the very beginning and it is why he sent his Son to earth (John 1:14). 'For God so loved the world that he gave his one and only Son, that whoever believes in him shall not perish but have eternal life' (John 3:16). That's the 'big story' of the Bible.

APPLY   How do you feel when you think of heaven? How does it affect the way you worship and the way you live now?

PRAY   Thank you, God, that some day there will be no more death or mourning or crying or pain, and I will worship you with all your saints in the New Jerusalem. Come Lord Jesus!

REVELATION: REVIEW

From the five readings in this section, summarise any significant insights and any thoughts on applying them to your life.

1

_____

_____

_____

2

_____

_____

_____

3

_____

_____

_____

4

_____

_____

_____

5

_____

_____

_____

Before you begin each new section you may find it helpful to read through your previous Review pages as a reminder of what God has been teaching you.

PRAYER JOURNAL

Prayer requests

Date: _____

_____

Date: _____

_____

Date: _____

_____

Date: _____

_____

Answered prayer

Date: _____

_____

Date: _____

_____

Date: _____

_____

PRAYER JOURNAL

Prayer requests

Date: _____

_____

Date: _____

_____

Date: _____

_____

Date: _____

_____

Answered prayer

Date: _____

_____

Date: _____

_____

Date: _____

_____

Date: _____

_____

PRAYER JOURNAL

Prayer requests

Date: _____

_____

Date: _____

_____

Date: _____

_____

Date: _____

_____

Answered prayer

Date: _____

_____

Date: _____

_____

Date: _____

_____

PRAYER JOURNAL

Prayer requests

Date: _____

_____

Date: _____

_____

Date: _____

_____

Date: _____

_____

Answered prayer

Date: _____

_____

Date: _____

_____

Date: _____

_____

Date: _____

_____

Beginning a relationship with God

As you discover in **Essential 100**, the 'big story' of the Bible is that God created a way for you to be free of your sin and to have a real relationship with him. That way is Jesus Christ.

As the apostle John wrote at the end of his Gospel, 'But these are written that you may believe that Jesus is the Christ, the Son of God, and that by believing you may have life in his name' (John 20:31). Putting your faith in Jesus is the only way to have a relationship with God. It is also the way to enjoy the benefits of the new life God offers you in Christ. Here's what that involves:

Eternal life Jesus conquered death and came back to life. He gives life that lasts forever to everyone who has faith in him: 'For God so loved the world that he gave his one and only Son, that whoever believes in him shall not perish but have eternal life' (John 3:16).

Meaningful life Jesus said, 'I came so that everyone would have life, and have it fully' (John 10:10b). God wants your life to be fulfilling, and Jesus can give you both purpose and fulfilment.

Guilt-free life All of us have done things that are wrong. The Bible calls this sin. Sin separates us from God. But God offers us forgiveness through Jesus Christ. John wrote in his first letter, 'But if we confess our sins to God, he can always be trusted to forgive us and take our sins away' (1 John 1:9).

New life 'But to all who believed him and accepted him, he gave the right to become children of God' (John 1:12). God created us to have a special, close relationship with him, just as a child has with a loving parent. This new relationship with God is available to you through Jesus.

How can I have faith in Jesus?

Faith in Jesus is:

- *Admitting* that I can't get to heaven or have new life on my own because I have sinned and my sins have separated me from God.
- *Believing* that Jesus is the Son of God who died on the cross to pay for my sins and give me new life.
- *Deciding* to follow Jesus for the rest of my life.

Here's a simple prayer that you might say to God, to tell him that you would like to receive the gift of new life offered by Jesus, his Son.

> Dear God, I admit that I've done wrong things and that my sin has separated me from you. I believe you sent Jesus to earth to die for the sins of the world – including mine – and that you brought him back to life again. Lord Jesus, as of right now, I'm deciding to follow you every day. Holy Spirit, I ask for your help to live a new life. Amen.

About your new life

Living life the way God intended it to be – to its fullest – means a daily relationship with him and with others who have new life in Christ. Here are some things that God wants us to do to make our relationships grow:

Talk to God That means prayer. You can talk to God any time, either silently or out loud. God wants to hear from you. You can tell him what you think of him, thank him for things, ask him for things for yourself or others.

Listen to God The main way God talks to us is through his book, the Bible. Reading the Bible can help you get to know God better and understand how he wants you to live. After you have completed **Essential 100**, you can get more help in reading, understanding, and applying the Bible from Scripture Union. See the next page for more information.

Join others who follow Jesus The Christian life is not just a personal thing. God wants you to join other followers of Jesus. The best place to do that is in a church where the people love Jesus and believe the Bible. There you can find a place to belong, to serve and be served, and to grow in your relationship with God.

Tell others When you get a great new gift, you want to tell other people. Go ahead; share the best gift in the world – Jesus Christ. Don't be pushy. Just tell people what God has done in your life and trust him do the rest.

God bless you!

BIBLE READING – WHAT NEXT?

Scripture Union aims to help people meet God and grow in personal relationship with him through Bible reading and prayer.

We produce a wide variety of resources for individuals and small groups, including:

WordLive: an innovative online Bible experience for groups and individuals, offering a wide variety of free material: study notes, maps, illustrations, images, poems, meditations, downloadable podcasts, prayer activities. Log on and check it out: www.wordlive.org

Daily Bread: helps you enjoy, explore and apply the Bible. Practical comments relate the Bible to everyday life.

Closer to God: a creative and reflective approach to Bible reading with an emphasis on renewal.

Encounter with God: for the more experienced Bible reader, providing a thought-provoking, in-depth approach to the Bible.

Essential Jesus by Whitney Kuniholm: 100-reading overview of the person and work of Jesus with notes and helps – a programme for individuals, small groups or whole churches.

The *LifeBuilder* series: small group study material. Many titles including topical and character studies, Old and New Testament books.

Resources for use with the E100 programme – including group and sermon outlines – are available from www.e100challenge.org.uk.

SU also produces Bible reading resources for children, teens and young adults. Do ask for details.

SU publications are available from Christian bookshops, on the Internet, or via mail order.

- Log on to www.scriptureunion.org.uk/shop.
- Phone SU's mail order line: 0845 07 06 006.
- Email: info@scriptureunion.org.uk.
- Write to SU Mail Order, PO Box 5148, Milton Keynes MLO, MK2 2YX.

Scripture Union

Using the Bible to inspire children, young people and adults to know God.